*M*ATLAB for *A*LL *E*ngineers

MATLAB Program for Engineering
Implementations
*E*xamples and *P*rogramming *L*ayout

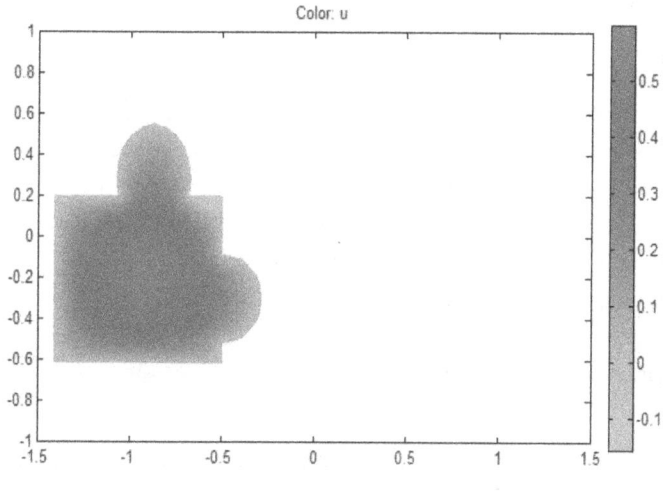

By

Eng. Saeed J. Almalowi
Mechanical Engineer
1st edition-2010

Rev. date: 01/22/2022

To order additional copies of this book, contact:
Xlibris
844-714-8691
www.Xlibris.com
Orders@Xlibris.com
566303

This book is about the *MATLAB* program for Engineering applications. It has lots of examples and explanations. Many computer programs help engineering students to modify and design different problems especially the problems that need more calculations. Therefore, it helps students to calculate a variety of implementations such as matrices, multiplications, for loops, design of amplifiers, and so on. All engineering students must use a computer program to design and analyze their projects. The goal of this book is to simplify the *MATLAB* program by using a variety of examples and explanations. It starts with simple and easy examples and then tries to go through more sophisticated examples.

Students should learn fundamental expressions before they start programming, so the book uses different explanations to help students to build up a strong understanding about this program. My goal is to help students to understand this type of program and also to help students to use this program in their projects. This book contains seven chapters; each includes examples and explanations. I hope this book helps lots of students who are looking for a thorough and easy *MATLAB* book. Indeed, I taught a *MATLAB* course for one semester in the College of Engineering at Tiabah University for Electrical Engineering students. I think it is an important computer language for all engineers to know how deal with this computer software.

Saeed J. Almalowi
Revised on 07/23/2014

CHAPTER#1: MATLAB Windows

1.1 Starting Windows

Two types of windows which are important to be known by users: command window and editor window/ or M-file window (script).

1.2. Commands Window

It allows users to correct their program's errors and helps them to figure out which types of errors programmers might have in their programs.

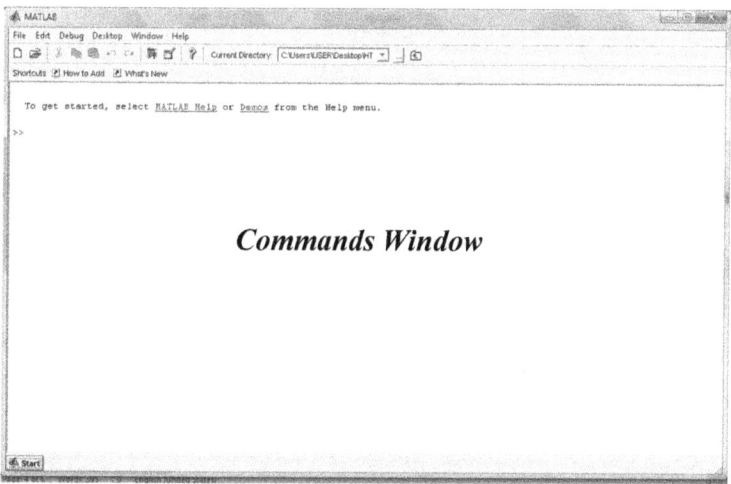

1.3. Editor Windows or M-File Windows

This window is used to build up a program. It is called M-File or script file .A programmer should be "save as" his file before starting

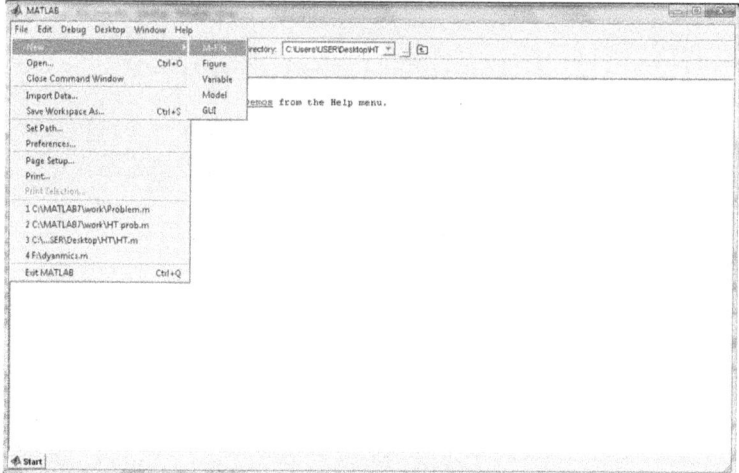

Save as an M-file and see this window

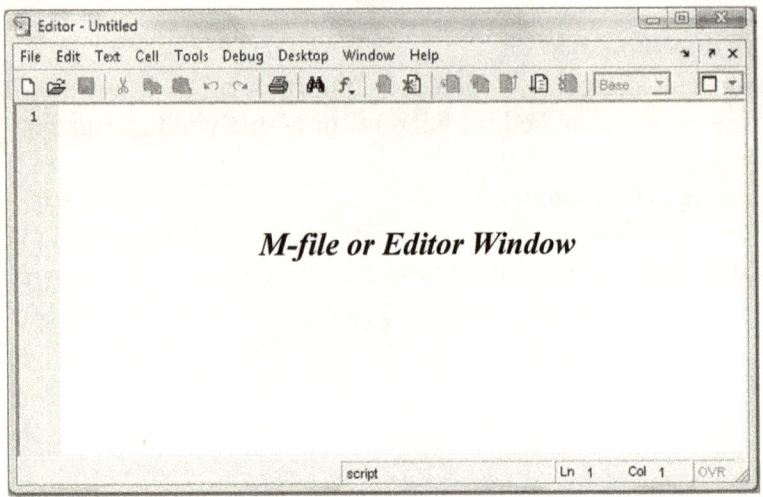

After opening MATLAB window, you might start your program or writing your commands.

CHAPTER#2:   Programming of Mathematical Problems and Functions

2.1. A mathematical and *MATLAb* Functions

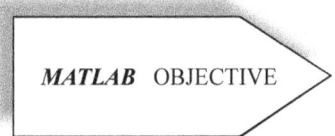

MATLAB Program is used to
- solve algebraic Equations
- know how to plot functions.
- solve differential equations,
- compute the integrals, and
- generate numerical solution of ODEs.

Mathematic Function Form	MATLAB Form
Square root $\sqrt{x}$	sqrt(x)
Exponential $e(x)$	exp(x)
logarithmic $\ln(x)$	log(x)
Logarithmic tenth $\log_{10}(x)$	Log10(x)
Sine angle $(\sin(\theta))$	$\sin(\theta)$
Cosine angle $(\cos(\theta))$	$\cos(\theta)$
Pie π	pi
Tan inverse angle $\tan^{-1}(\theta)$	$a\tan(\theta)$
Subtract -	-
Adding +	+
Power	^
Division $\div$	/
Multiple	*

MATLAB logic operators will be discussed in the following chapter.

2.2. Adding and Subtracting

Example (1): Add the following mathematical calculations

a- 4+5-10
b- 3+10+50-23
c- 5+ (-1)+4-3
d- 5+100+567-234

Ans.

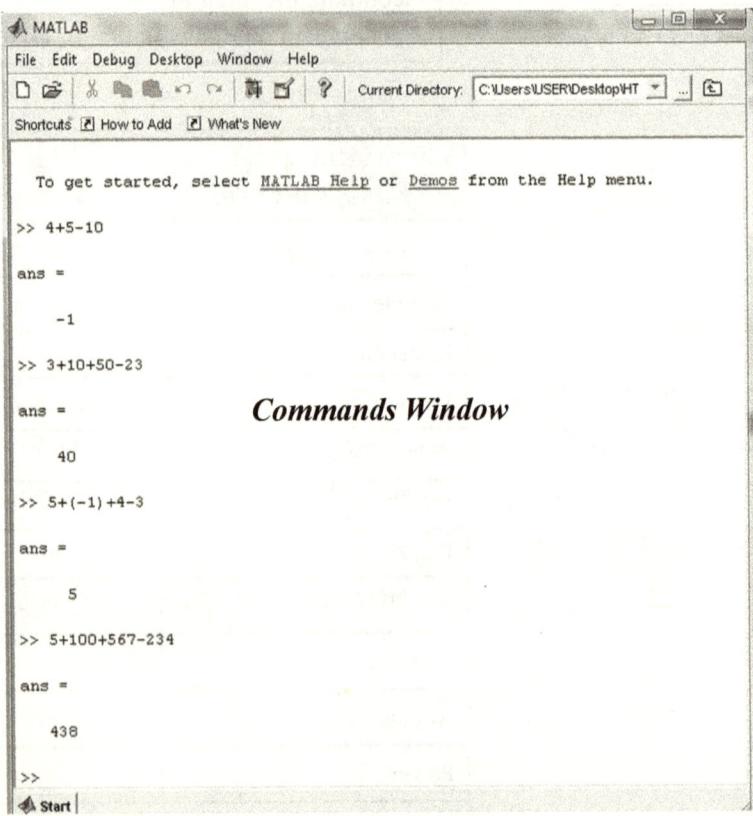

2.3 Multiplication and Division (* and /)

Example (2): Estimate the following mathematical calculations

a- $4\times5\div5+3\times6$
b- $4\times0\div10+12$
c- $10\times234+25$
d-$(5\div8\div7)\times5$

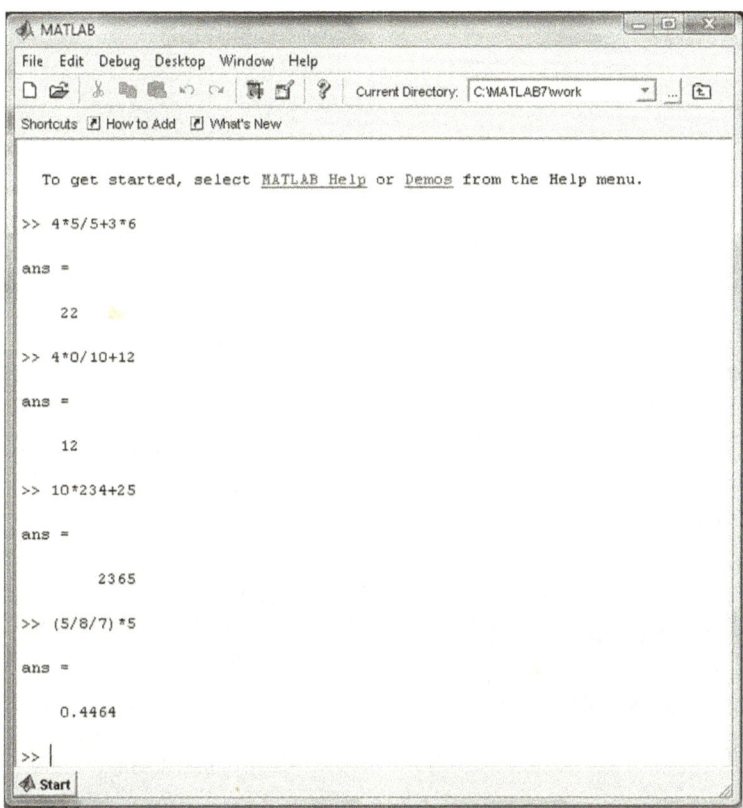

Example (3): Estimate the following calculations
a- $4\times((5\div6)+(3\div2))$
b- $6\times(100^3+5\div4)$
c- $(4^5)^{6-2}$
d- $15-23+45+100^{45}$

Ans.

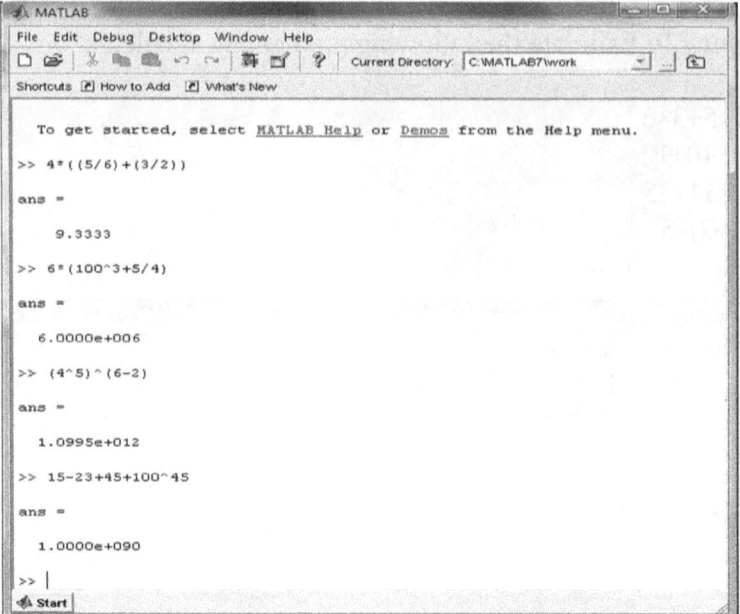

By hand

4×((5÷6)+(3÷2))

First of all, this operation is calculated from inside the parenthesis from left to right. Then multiply by the outside number.

Step #: (5÷6) =(0.833)

Step#2: (3÷2) = (1.5)

Step#3: (Step#1+Step#2) = (0.833+1.5)=(2.333)

Step#4: 4×(Step#3) = 4×(2.333) = 9.333

2.4. Basic Triangle Functions

Right hand triangle

$$tan\theta = \frac{H}{L} \quad\quad cos\theta = \frac{L}{x} \quad\quad sin\theta = \frac{H}{x}$$

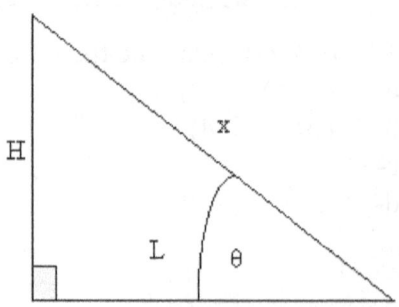

Example (4): Estimate the basic triangle expressions and the other mathematical expressions

a- πb- $\sqrt{27}$
c- $24^{(34-2)}$
d- sin(90)
e- tan(45)
f- $25 - \sqrt{\cos(60)}$

Ans.

```
Shortcuts  [#] How to Add  [#] What's New

>> pi

ans =

      3.1416

>> sqrt(27)

ans =

      5.1962

>> 24^(34-2)

ans =

   1.4681e+044

>> sin(pi/2)

ans =

      1

>> tan(pi/3)

ans =

      1.7321

>> 25-sqrt(cos(pi/3))

ans =

      24.2929

Start
```

2.5. Vectors and Matrices

The vectors are a part of matrices. They are structured either in rows or columns. Therefore, the matrices are a group of rows and columns of vectors. Showing rows and vectors by using MATLAB have different commands, so in this section will be learning the matrices structures.

Example (5): Create the column vector with three elements

Ans.

$$A = \begin{bmatrix} 1 \\ 2 \\ 3 \end{bmatrix}$$

\>>A=[1; 2 ; 3]
ans=

   1
   2
   3

Example (6): Create the row vector with three elements

Ans.
B=[1 2 3]
\>>B=[1, 2, 3]
ans=
   1 2 3

2.5.1. Transpose the Vector

The column vectors can be turned into the row vectors by using "Á" . As we know a vector which has elements in a row will be in the horizontal, but a vector which has elements in column will be in the vertical.

A is the vector in one column and three rows. $A = \begin{bmatrix} 1 \\ 2 \\ 3 \end{bmatrix}$

B is the Vector in one row and three columns. $B = [1\ 3\ 4]$

Therefore, matrices have number of rows and columns.

Square Matrices (SM)
C is the square matrix because it has three rows and three columns.

$$C = \begin{bmatrix} 1 & 3 & 4 \\ 5 & 6 & 8 \\ 10 & 12 & 14 \end{bmatrix}$$

The reverse of this matrix will be "Ć"

A square matrix means that the numbers of rows are equal to the numbers of columns.

Example (7): Find the reverse vector for the following vectors

$$A = [1\ 2\ 3], B = \begin{bmatrix} 2 \\ 6 \\ 7 \end{bmatrix}$$

Ans.

Example (8): create the following matrix, and then find the reverse of the matrix, too.

$$C = \begin{bmatrix} 1 & 3 & 4 \\ 5 & 6 & 8 \\ 10 & 12 & 14 \end{bmatrix}$$

Ans.

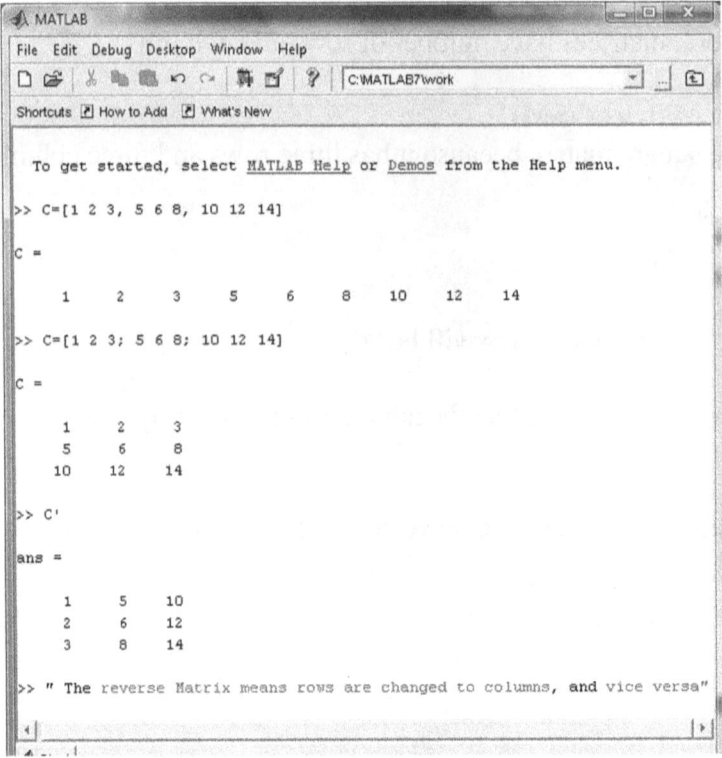

Notice: see in this window the colon makes the matrix in row, but the semi- colon makes the matrix in rows and columns as it is required in the example(8).

Rectangular Matrices (RM)

RM is the number of columns more than the numbers of rows or vice versa.

$$\begin{bmatrix} 1235 \\ 4567 \\ 8\ 986 \end{bmatrix}$$ This is called the rectangular matrix.

Diagonal Matrices (DM)

A first element of the first row is 1, the second element of the second row is 1, and the third element of the third row is 1 for SM.

$$\begin{bmatrix} 100 \\ 010 \\ 001 \end{bmatrix}$$

Unit Matrices (UM)
All elements are one.

$$\begin{bmatrix} 1111 \\ 1111 \\ 1111 \end{bmatrix}$$

Zero Matrices (ZM)
All the elements of this type of matrices are zeros.

$$\begin{bmatrix} 000 \\ 000 \\ 000 \end{bmatrix}$$

Examples (9) create the zero, diagonal, and unit matrices by using MATLAB command window.

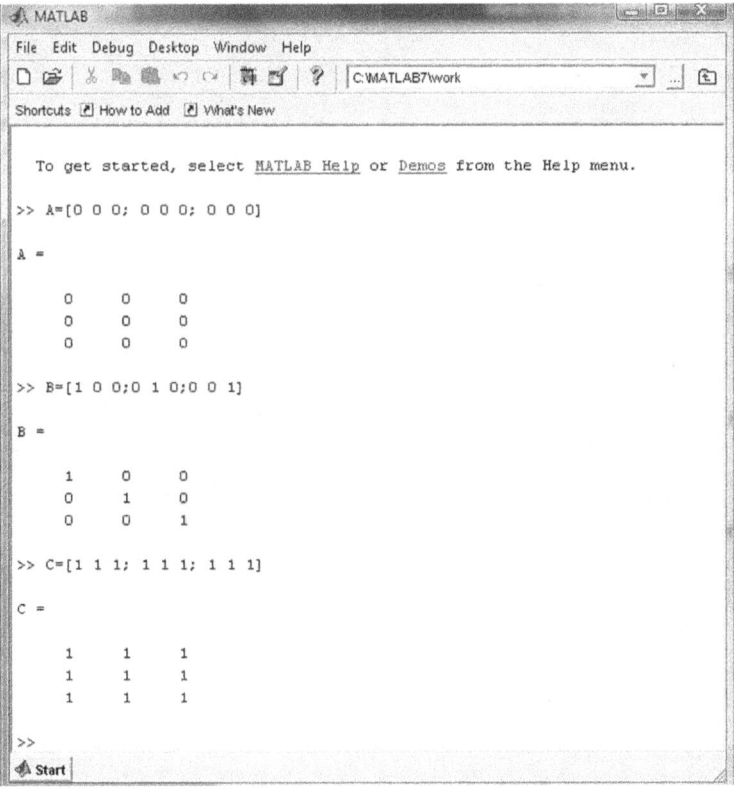

2.6 Vectors Rules and Adding of Matrices, Subtracting of Matrices, and multiplication of Matrices

2.6.1. Adding and subtracting vectors

In order to add vectors or subtract vectors, they must have must same of rows and columns. We cannot add a vector which has two rows with a vector which has three rows.

Example (10): Add the following vectors
1. A= [1 2 3], B= [3 4 5], C=A+B
2. A= [1 2], B=[3 4 5], C=A+B
3.
$$A = \begin{bmatrix} 1 \\ 2 \\ 3 \end{bmatrix}, B = \begin{bmatrix} 3 \\ 4 \\ 5 \end{bmatrix}, C = A + B$$

```
A MATLAB                                                    _ □ X

File  Edit  Debug  Desktop  Window  Help

D ☞ | ✂ ▣ ▣ ▫ ▫ | ▦ ▣ | ? |  C:\MATLAB7\work          ▼ ... ⟐

Shortcuts ▣ How to Add  ▣ What's New


    To get started, select MATLAB Help or Demos from the Help menu.

>> A=[1 2 3];
>> B=[3 4 5];
>> C=A+B

C =

      4      6      8

>> A=[1 2];
>> B=[3 4 5];
>> C=A+B
??? Error using ==> plus
Matrix dimensions must agree.

>> A=[1;2;3];
>> B=[3;4;5];
>> C=A+B

C =

      4
      6
      8

>> |
A Start
```

Example (11): Subtract the following vectors

1. A= [1 2 3], B= [3 4 5], C=A-B
2. A= [1 2], B=[3 4 5], C=A-B
3.
$$A = \begin{bmatrix} 1 \\ 2 \\ 3 \end{bmatrix}, B = \begin{bmatrix} 3 \\ 4 \\ 5 \end{bmatrix}, C = A - B$$

Ans.

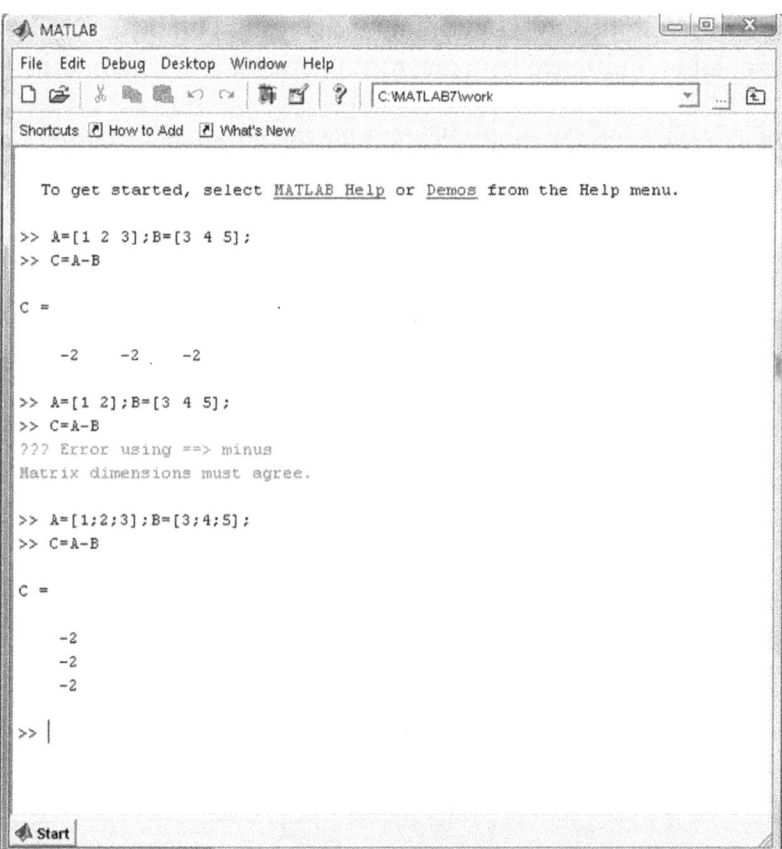

2.6.2 Multiplication and division vectors

N is the number of rows, and m is the number of columns.
3×2 means N=3 and m=2; therefore, the N×m can be multiplied in each other's if N in the first vector is equal to m in the second vector.

Explanation:

$$A = [12\ 3], B = \begin{bmatrix} 3 \\ 4 \\ 5 \end{bmatrix}, N_A = m_B \text{ or } N_B = m_A$$

In the first vector $N \times m = (1 \times 3)$, but in the second vector is opposite $N \times m = (3 \times 1)$

Consequently, $N_A = m_B$ and vice versa. (Rule#2)

Notice:

A one row multiplied by a one column, the result will be a one value.
A one column multiplied by a one row, the result will be a matrix.

Example (12): Find the multiplication for the following vectors.

$$A = [12\ 3], B = \begin{bmatrix} 3 \\ 4 \\ 5 \end{bmatrix}, C = BxA$$

$$A = [12\ 3], B = \begin{bmatrix} 3 \\ 4 \\ 5 \end{bmatrix}, C = AxB$$

The rules of the division are not the same as the rules of the multiplications.
$N_A = N_B$ and $m_A = m_B$

There is another type of commands which can be used to flip or reshape a matrix.

MATLAB commands	Meaning
C=reshape(A,N,m)	To returns the m-by-n matrix C whose elements are taken column-wise from A
flipud(A)	To flip a matrix from up to bottom.
fliprl(A)	To flip a matrix from right to left.
fliplr(A)	To flip a matrix from left to right.

Example (13): Divide the following vectors:

$$A = \begin{bmatrix} 12 & 3 \end{bmatrix}, B = \begin{bmatrix} 3 \\ 4 \\ 5 \end{bmatrix}, C = A/B$$

$$A = \begin{bmatrix} 12 & 3 \end{bmatrix}, B = \begin{bmatrix} 3 \\ 4 \\ 5 \end{bmatrix}, C = B/A$$

Ans.

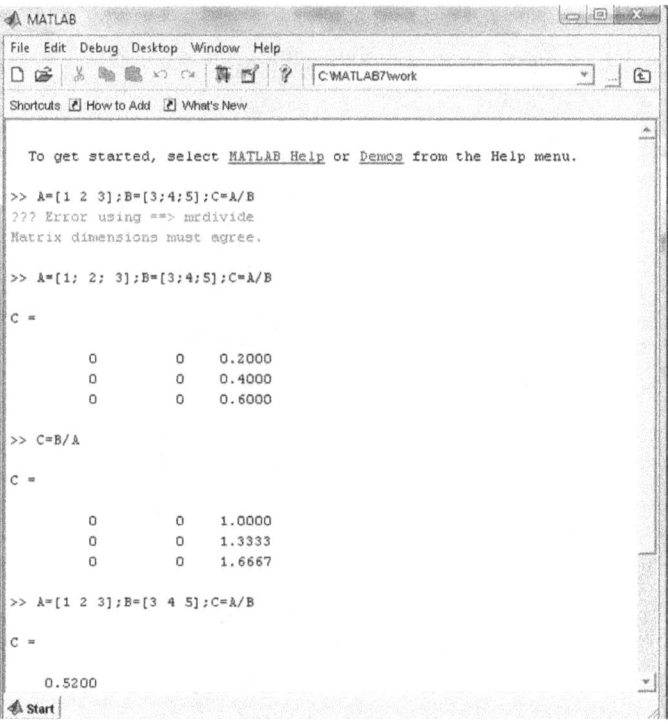

2.6.3. The matrices Rules

Matrices have different rules which are based on type of matrix and type of the mathematical operation (+, *,-, /).

2.6.3.1. Adding and subtracting matrices

The two matrices must be the same type (SM-SM, SM+SM, RM-RM, RM+RM....etc)

2.6.3.1 Multiplication and division of matrices

The multiplication of matrices has different rules. We can multiply a row vector in a matrix, but we cannot multiply a matrix in a row vector

We can multiply SM in SM, and we cannot multiply RM in SM, we cannot multiply SM in RM, as well.

Examples (14): find the following expressions

$$A = \begin{bmatrix} 12\ 3 \\ 3\ 4\ 5 \\ 67\ 8 \end{bmatrix}, B = \begin{bmatrix} 3 \\ 4 \\ 5 \end{bmatrix}, C = A \times B, C = B \times A$$

$$A = \begin{bmatrix} 12\ 3 \\ 34\ 5 \\ 6\ 78 \end{bmatrix}, B = \begin{bmatrix} 3\ 7\ 9 \\ 4\ 6\ 9 \\ 5\ 01 \end{bmatrix}, C = A \times B, C = B \times A$$

Ans.

```
Shortcuts  How to Add   What's New
    To get started, select MATLAB Help or Demos from the Help menu.

>> A=[1 2 3; 3 4 5; 6 7 8]; B=[3 4 5];
>> C=A*B
??? Error using ==> mtimes
Inner matrix dimensions must agree.

>> C=B*A

C =

     45    57    69

>> A=[1 2 3; 3 4 5; 6 7 8]; B=[3 7 9; 4 6 9; 5 0 1];
>> C=A*B

C =

     26    19    30
     50    45    68
     86    84   125

>> C=B*A

C =

     78    97   116
     76    95   114
     11    17    23

>> |
 Start
```

Division of Two Matrices

We can divide two matrices under certain rules. We can divide the same type of matrices, for instance, RM/RM, SM/SM....etc.

Example (15):

```
To get started, select MATLAB Help or Demos from the Help menu.

>> A=[1 2 3; 3 4 5; 6 7 8]; B=[3 7 9; 4 6 9; 5 0 1];
>> C=A/B

C =

   -0.0571    0.4000   -0.0857
    0.9143   -0.4000    0.3714
    2.3714   -1.6000    1.0571

>> C=B/A
Warning: Matrix is close to singular or badly scaled.
         Results may be inaccurate. RCOND = 2.114711e-018.

C =

  1.0e+016 *

   -0.6755    1.1259   -0.4504
    0.3378   -0.5629    0.2252
    2.0266   -3.3777    1.3511

>>
```

We can divide a vector on a matrix and vice versa. Further, we can divide RM on SM and vice versa. All those rules should be considered by a programmer before he/ she creates his/her program. A professional programmer must know all of those rules to design any type of program. MATLAB helps a programmer to figure out his mistakes. The mistakes will show up in the command window.

Tracing any column or row in a matrix A
A(1,:) takes the first column in a matrix A.
A(n,:) takes "n" values of a "n" row.
A(:,n) takes "n" values of a "n" column.

Shortcuts ? How to Add   ? What's New

```
    To get started, select MATLAB Help or Demos from the Help menu.

>> A=[1 2 3]; B=[3 7 9; 4 6 9; 5 0 1];
>> C=A/B

C =

   -0.0571     0.4000    -0.0857

>> C=B/A

C =

    3.1429
    3.0714
    0.5714

>> A=[1 2 3;3 4 5; 6 7 8; 9 0 2]; B=[3 7 9; 4 6 9; 5 0 1];
>> C=A/B

C =

   -0.0571     0.4000    -0.0857
    0.9143    -0.4000     0.3714
    2.3714    -1.6000     1.0571
   -0.1714     0.2000     1.7429

>> C=B/A

C =

    1.9091          0    0.4545    -0.1818
    2.7455          0    0.0727     0.0909
   -0.1273          0    0.0364     0.5455

>>
```

Start

Notice: We can divide one element on any type of matrix. Also, we can multiply one element by a matrix.

CHAPTER#3:   Plots and Functions

3.1. Plots of Mathematical Functions

Plots are important part which helps us to understand more about a problem. All engineers use those kinds of plots to figure out a solution. Plots should have x-label, y-label, and title. Therefore, in this chapter we will learn how to draw plot and add all labels and titles for any types of plots. Further, we will try to draw all types of plots.

3.1.2. Line Plot (command: plot
Example (16)

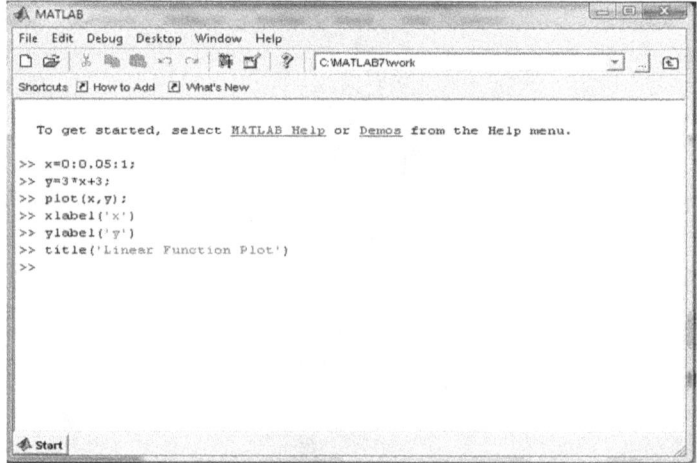

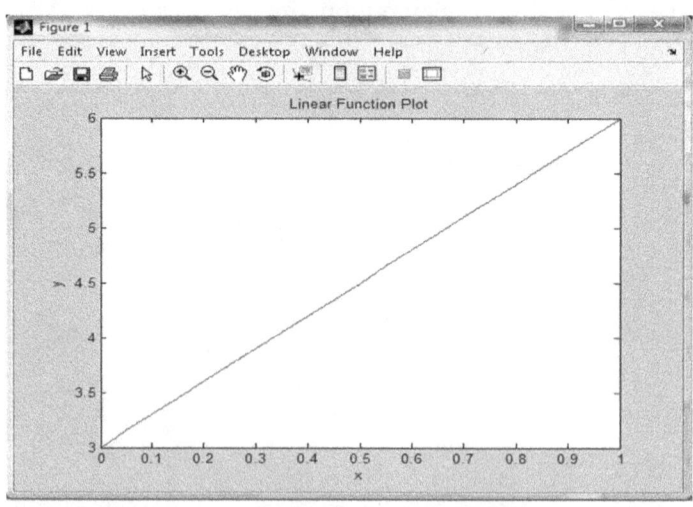

The entire of the program is

```
x=0:0.05:1;
y= 3*x+3;
plot(x,y);
xlabel('x');
ylabel('y');
title('Linear Equation Plot')
```

For practicing, you are able to copy this program and put it on the command window or M-file window.

Example (17)

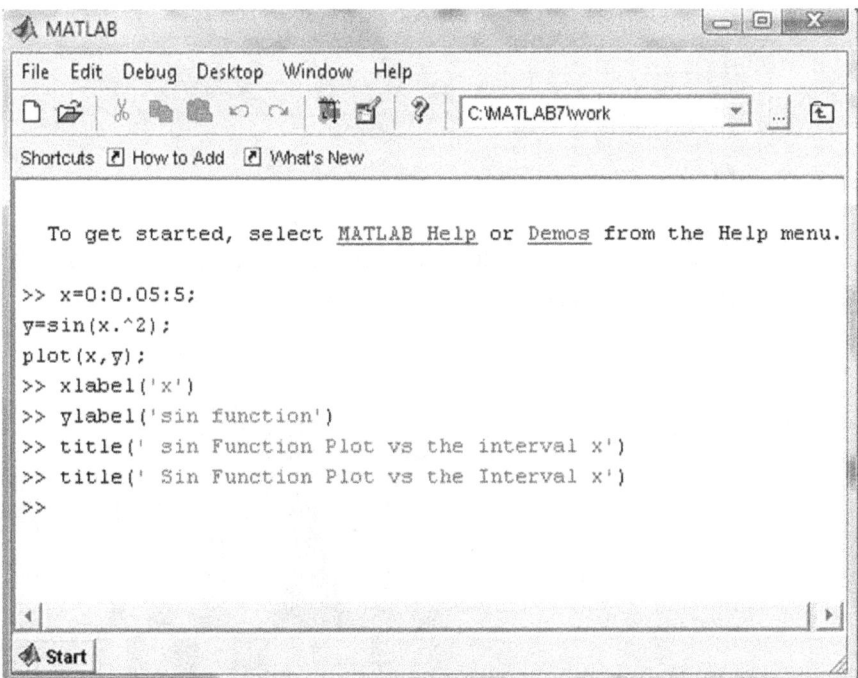

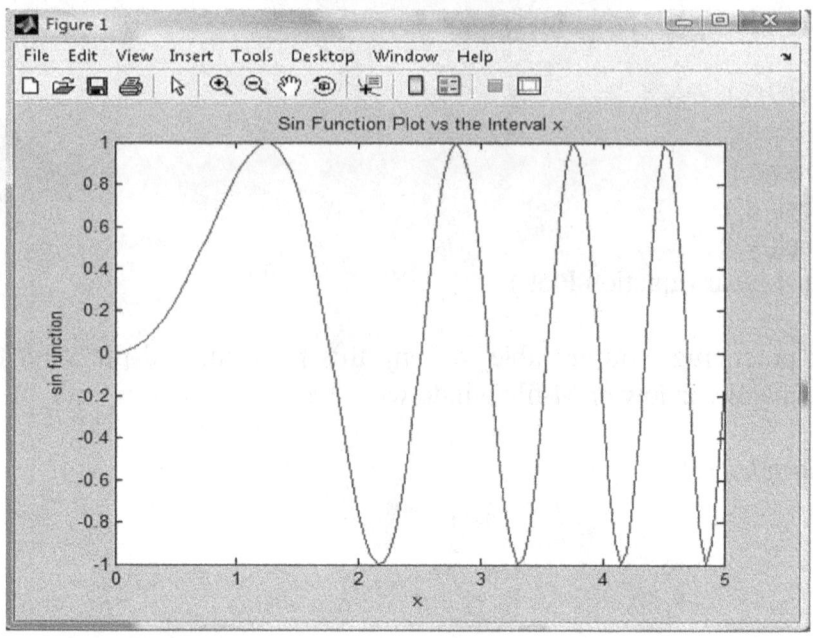

3.1.2. Bar Plot(command: bar)

A bar plot is the one type of a plot which is used to show statistical measuring or other usages.

Example (18)

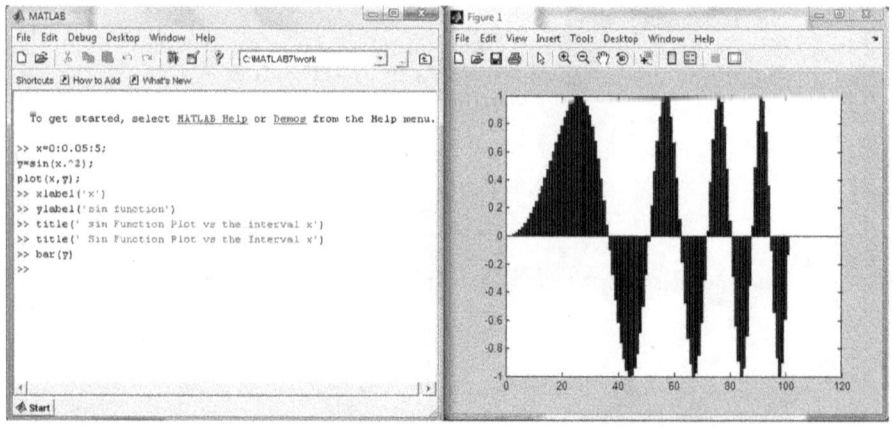

3.1.3. Stem plot (command: stem)

Example (19)

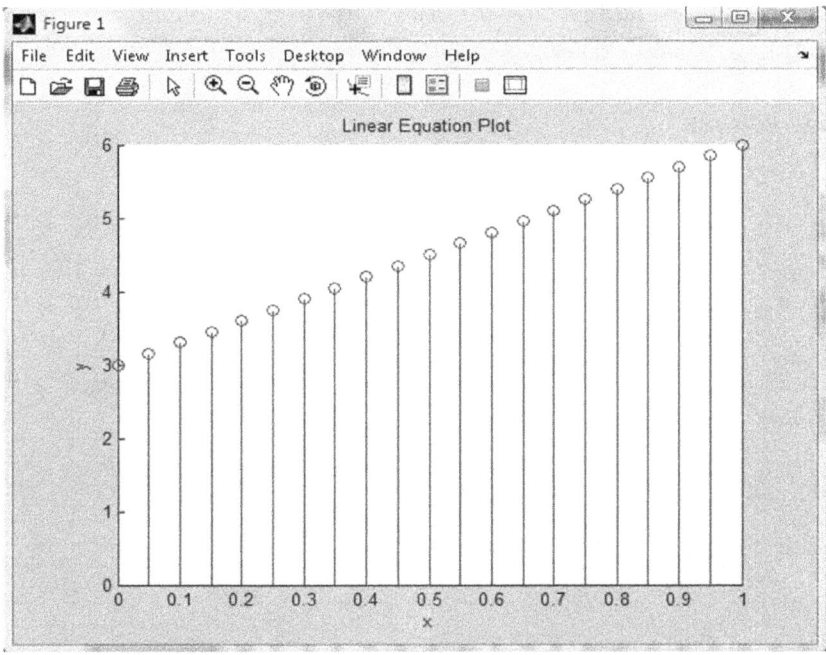

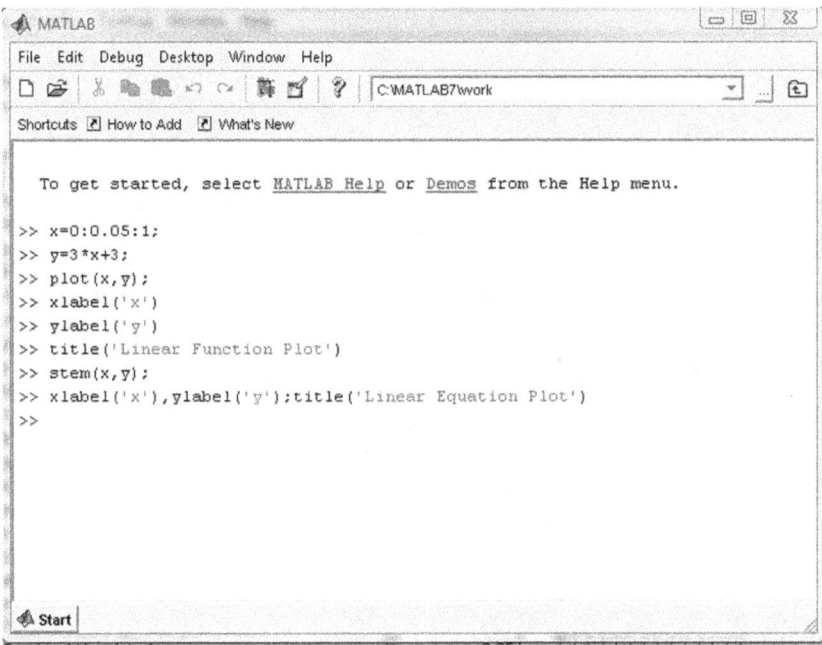

3.2. Linear Equations Functions with one variable (command: fzero (function))

Mathematical equations have different ways to be evaluated. First degree function with one variable is easy to solve.

Explanation:
3x-6=0
x=6/3=2

Example (19): Calculate π by finding the zero of the sine function near 4, and also find 2x-5=0
Ans.

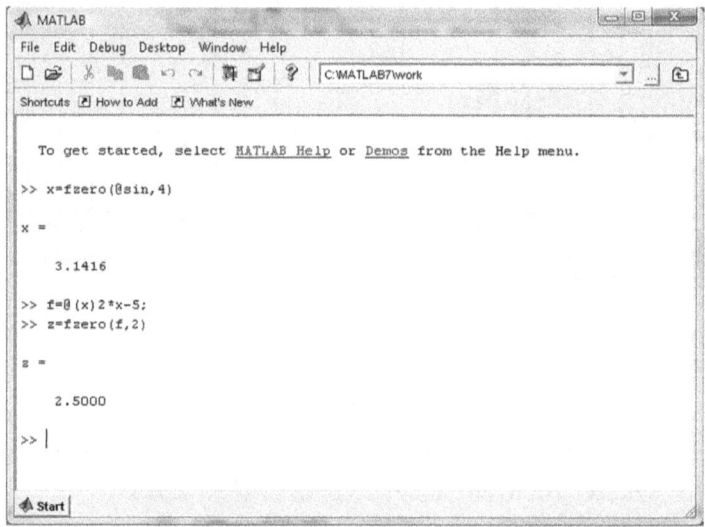

Notice: for the near value, you can choose the near value for zero. For example, 2x-5=0, we can choose 0, 1,2…etc. and we will get the same answer.

Example (20) : Evaluate the solution for the following function
4x+5x+27=0

>> z = fzero(@(x)4*x+5*x+27,1)

=z

-3.0000

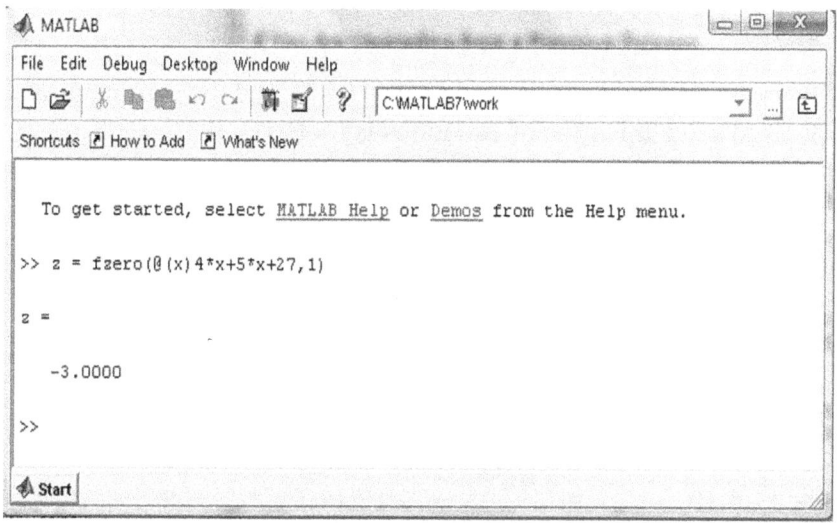

3.2.1a Second Degree Functions (command: root)

Solving the second degree equations are by using a quadratic 2nd order equation $ax^2+bx+c=0$

$$x = \frac{-b \pm \sqrt{b^2 - 4ac}}{2a}$$

Explanations:

$x^2+4x+4=0$, $(x+2)(x+2)=0$, so x =-2,-2, two values, multiplication of both of them is equal to 4 and adding both of them is equal to 4.
By using quadratic 2nd order solution formula

$$x = \frac{-4 \pm \sqrt{4^2 - 4 \times 1 \times 4}}{2} = -2, -2$$

By MATLAB

A "P" is the factors of unknown "x", P=[1 4 4], and the command which helps us to solve this type of equations is roots.

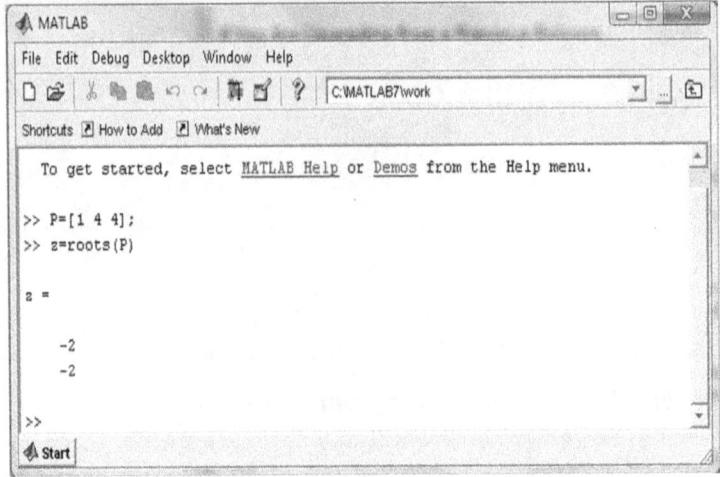

Example (21): Estimate the square roots of $3x^2+9x-27$.

Ans.

P= [3 9 -27];
z = roots(P)

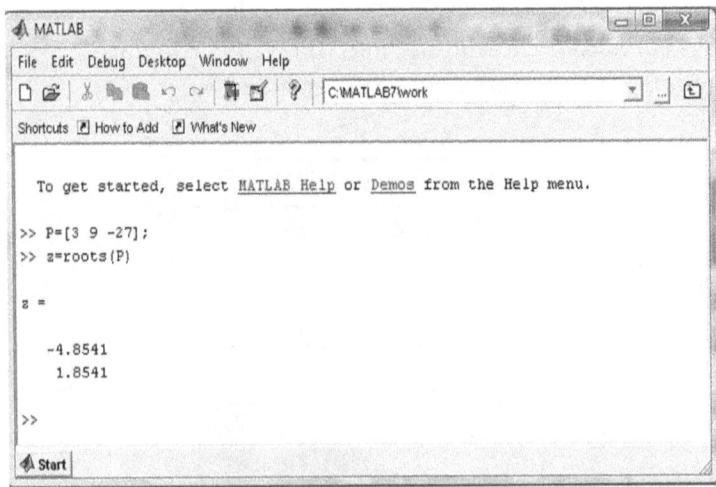

3.2.1b. Linear equations with two and three variables

Linear equations might have two or three variables (x,y,z), so we should know how to solve theose types of equations.

3.2.2a Linear Equations with two variables

Example (22): Estimate the values of x and y for the following equations

3x+4y=25
4x+6y=12

Ans.

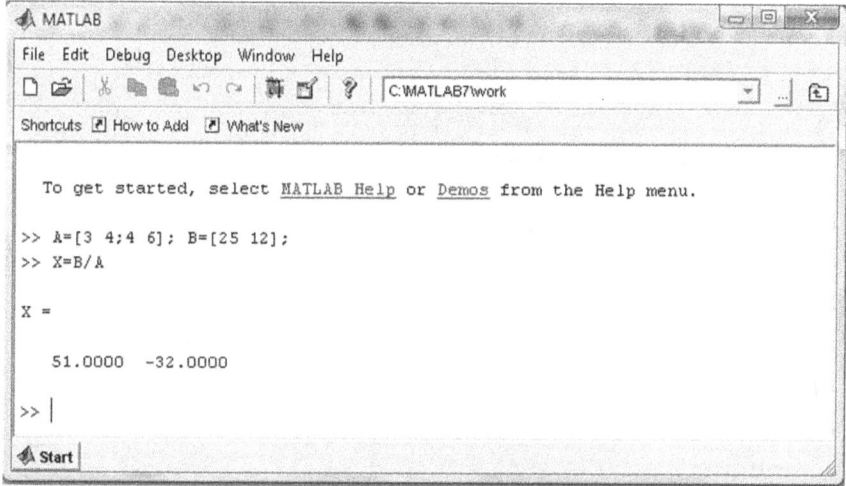

Explanations:
$AX = B$
$ax + by = k$
$cx + dy = m$
$$\begin{vmatrix} a & b \\ c & d \end{vmatrix}\begin{vmatrix} x \\ y \end{vmatrix} = \begin{vmatrix} k \\ m \end{vmatrix}$$

3.2.2b. Linear Equations with three variables

Example (23): Find the solutions of the following equations

$3x+4y+8z = 13$
$2 x + 5y+9z = -9$
$6 x+y =3$

To solve these equations, we have two methods. 1st method by using matrices AX=B and the 2nd method by using solve and syms commands
>> syms x y z;
>> [x,y,z]= solve (eq1,eq2,eq3)

Ans.

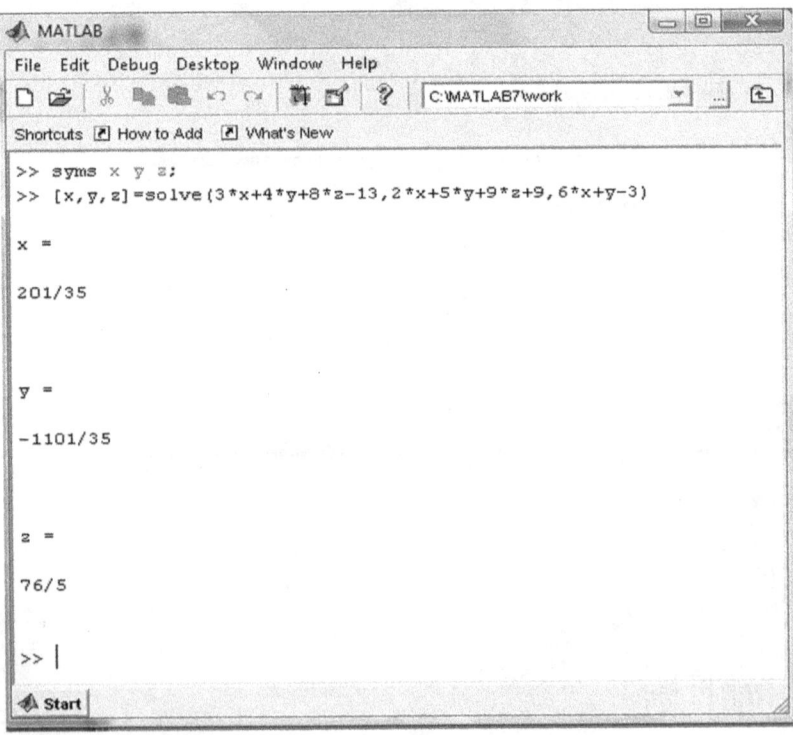

```
>> syms x y z;
>> [x,y,z]=solve(3*x+4*y+8*z-13,2*x+5*y+9*z+9,6*x+y-3)

x =

201/35


y =

-1101/35


z =

76/5


>> |
```

<u>Notice</u>: the values of x, y, and z are respectively.

3.4. Nonlinear Equations with, one variable, two variables and three variables.

A mathematical equation or function has different degree, for instance, 1st degree, 2nd degree, 3rd degree or nth degree. Therefore, we will mention all of those types of degrees.

3.4.1a. Nonlinear Equations with One Variable

$Y= ax^3+bx^2+cx+d$, we must find the value of x by using fzero command.

Example (24): Find the value of x for the following equation

$Y= 3x^3-2x^2+x+4$
Ans.

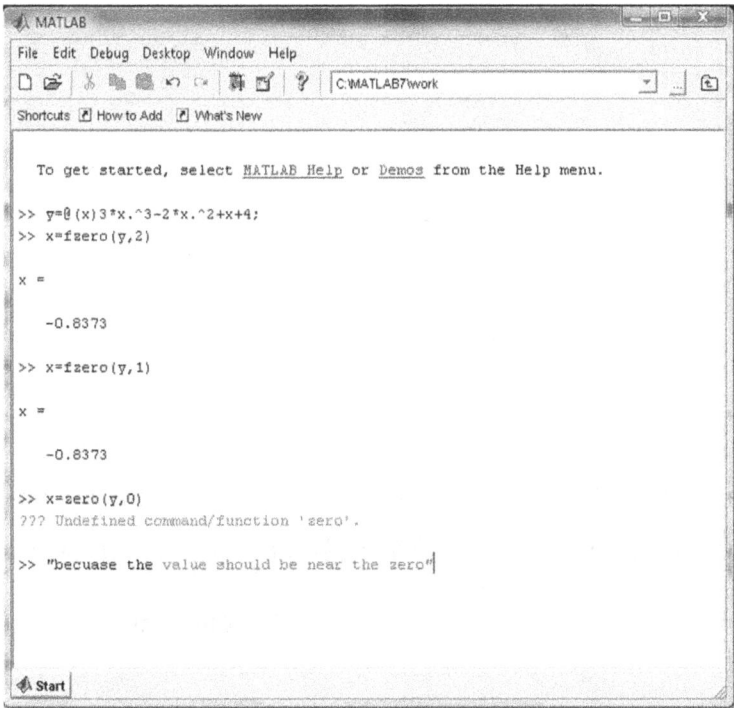

Checking if the answer is correct!?
Substitute in the original equation if the equation is equal to zero the value of the x is correct. Try by yourself.

3.4.1b. Nonlinear Equations with Two Variables (Command: syms, solve)

This section explains how to solve systems of equations using symbolic (syms) math and solve command.

$x^2+y^2=a$

$x+y=b$

Example (25): Find the solution of those mathematical functions

$x^2+y^2=10$

$x+y=3$

Ans.

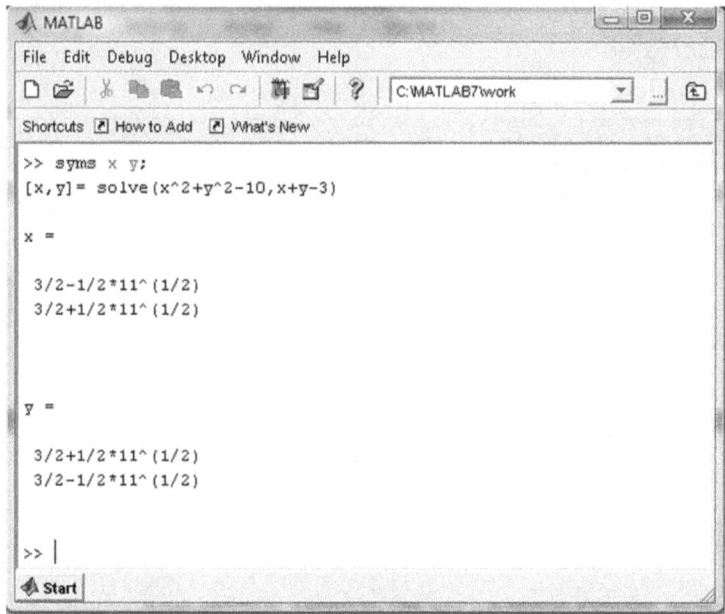

3.4.1c. Nonlinear Equations with three Variables (command: syms, solve)

Example (26): Determine the solution for the following equations

$x^2+y^2+z^2=23$

$5x^2+4y^2+3z^2=10$

$2x^2+6y^2=5$

Ans. it is awkward to solve those types of equations by hand, so we have to use a computer program to solve them. Also, we can use some types of calculation machine which might help students to solve those types of equations.

We will solve those equations by using "syms" and "solve" command. The solution of those equations does not take time to be solved with MATLAB, it takes a few seconds!!.

Ans

```
>> syms x y z;
[x,y,z]=solve(x^2+y^2+z^2-23,5*x^2+4*y^2+3*z^2-10,2*x^2+6*y^2-5)

x =

  1/10*i*3590^(1/2)
  1/10*i*3590^(1/2)
 -1/10*i*3590^(1/2)
 -1/10*i*3590^(1/2)
  1/10*i*3590^(1/2)
  1/10*i*3590^(1/2)
 -1/10*i*3590^(1/2)
 -1/10*i*3590^(1/2)


y =

  8/5*5^(1/2)
 -8/5*5^(1/2)
  8/5*5^(1/2)
 -8/5*5^(1/2)
  8/5*5^(1/2)
 -8/5*5^(1/2)
  8/5*5^(1/2)
 -8/5*5^(1/2)


z =

  1/10*4610^(1/2)
  1/10*4610^(1/2)
  1/10*4610^(1/2)
  1/10*4610^(1/2)
 -1/10*4610^(1/2)
 -1/10*4610^(1/2)
 -1/10*4610^(1/2)
 -1/10*4610^(1/2)

>>
```

3.4. The Trending Line and curve fitting

Command: "grid on" is used to draw a graphical sheet.

The trending curve and curve fitting is used if we have a data or if we need to create an equation for a group of data or to fit some data in reported or plotted data.

Example (27): the experiment shows data for the time and the velocity of fly as shown in this table:

Time (t) sec	0	0.3	0.8	1.1	1.6	2.3
Velocity (v) cm	0	0.5	0.8	1.14	1.26	1.4

Estimate the relationship between the time and the velocity of the fly (regression), draw chart.

grid on command

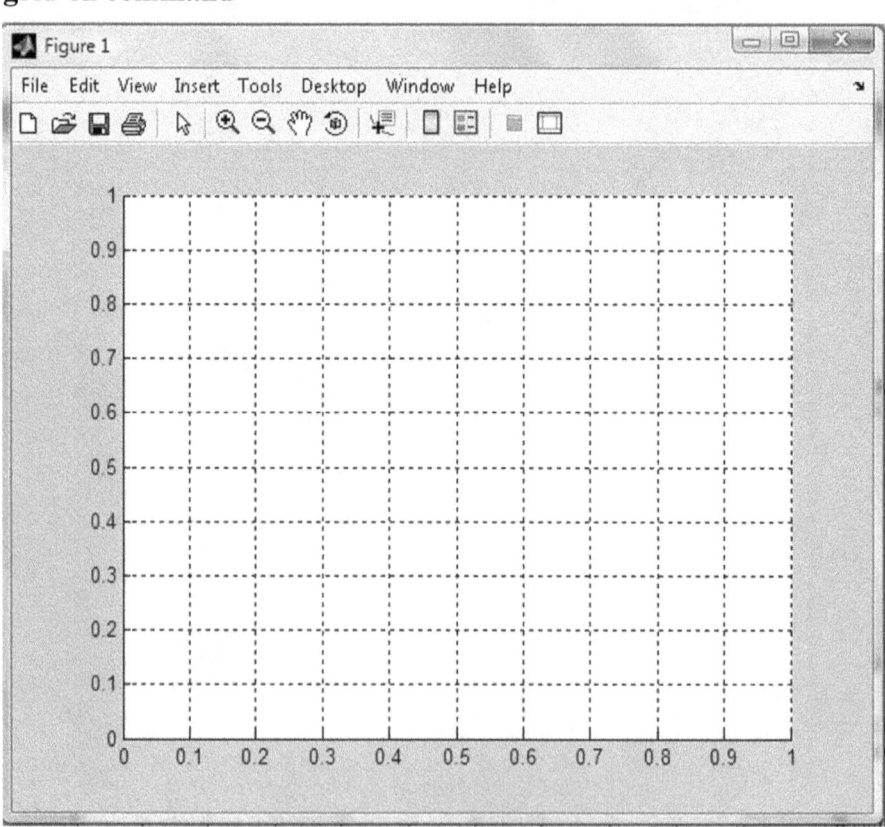

Ans.

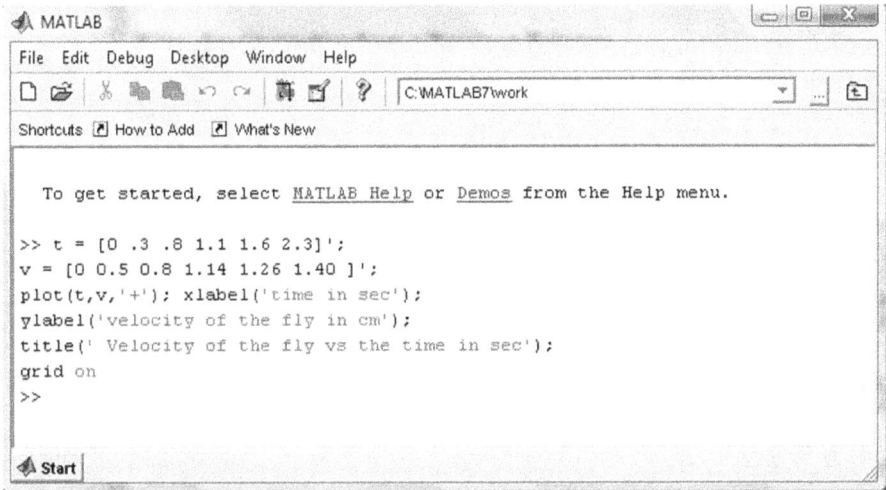

The chart

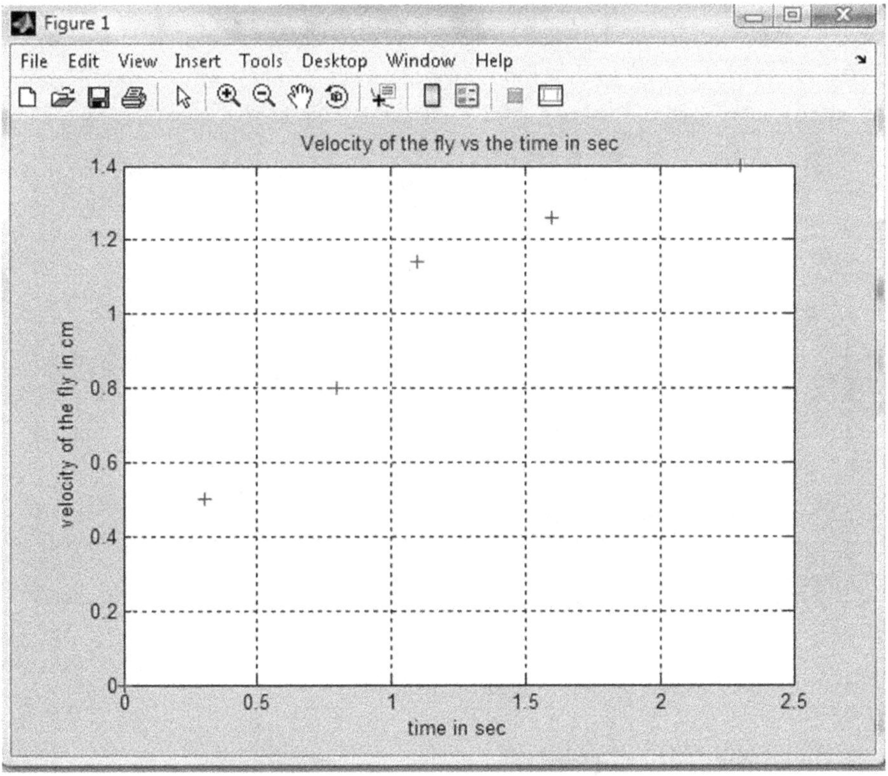

3.5.1a Backslash operator and Curve fitting (backslash operator is '\')

3.5.1a. Polynomial curve fitting (command: ones size(x))

$$y = a_0 + a_1 x_1 + a_2 x_2^2$$

For this equation we need to find the values of each factors, a_0, a_1, a_2.
X = [ones(size(x)) x x.^2]

$XA=Y$, $A= [a_0\ a_1\ a_2]$, $X =[x_1\ x_2]$

Example (28): Estimate the values of all factors of the following equation.

$$y = a_0 + a_1 x + a_2 x^2$$

x	0.2	0.8	0.5
y	0.11	0.6	0.3

Ans.

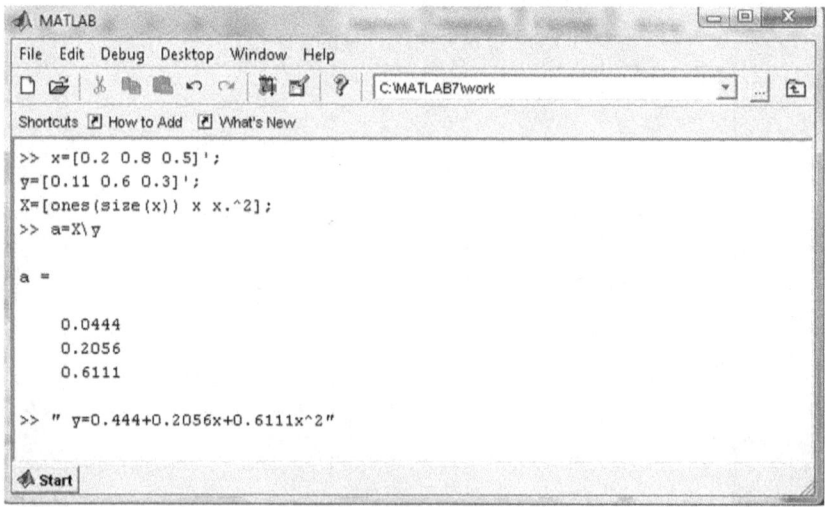

This method is called "least square method".

$$y = 0.044 + 0.2056x_1 + 0.6111x_2^2$$

To check this equation, substitute the value of x to get the value of y as they shown in the table.

Explanation:

At x=0.8 the value of y=0.6, so y $=0.044+0.2056\times0.8+0.6111\times(0.8)^2$ $=0.599 \approx 0.6$ (correct).

3.5.1b. Linear Regression with an Exponential Equation

$y = a_0 + a_1e^{-t} + a_2te^{-t}$

Example (29):

Estimate the values of factors for this equation:

$y = a_0 + a_1e^{-t} + a_2te^{-t}$

t	0.2	0.3	0.4	0.5	0.6
y	0.11	0.23	0.3	0.35	0.45

Ans.

```
>> t=[0.2 0.3 0.4 0.5 0.6]';
>> y=[0.11 0.23 0.3 0.35 0.45]';
>> X=[ones(size(t)) exp(-t) t.*exp(-t)];
>> a=X\y

a =

    0.9209
   -1.0313
    0.2538

>> T = (0:0.1:2.5)';
Y = [ones(size(T)) exp(-T)  T.*exp(-T)]*a;
plot(T,Y,'-',t,y,'o'), grid on
>>
```

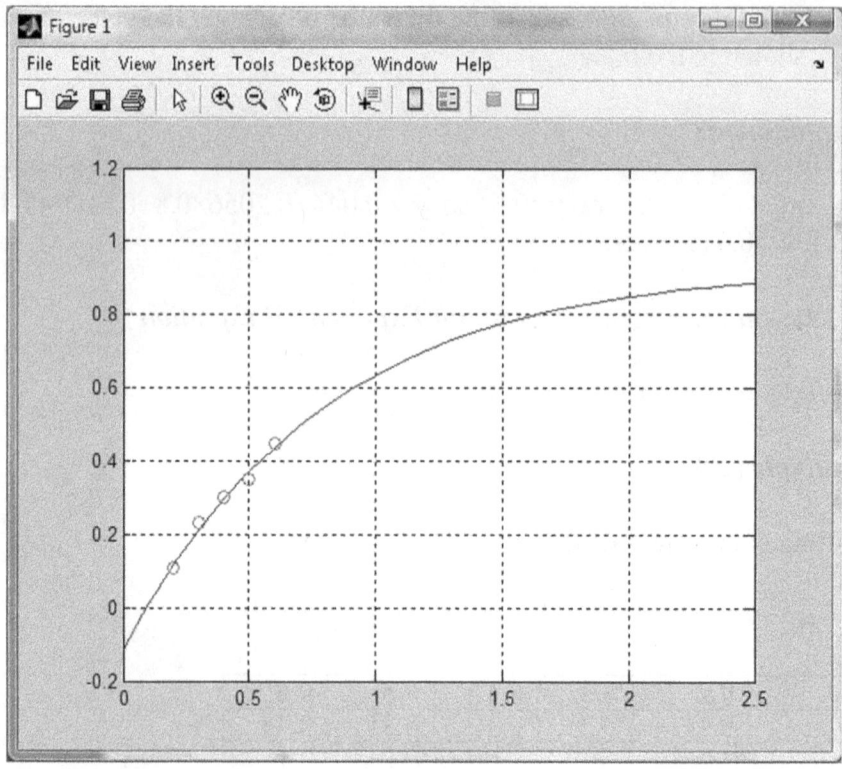

$y = 0.9209 - 1.0313e^{-t} + 0.2538te^{-t}$

3.5.1c Multiple Regression

Sometimes, Mathematical equations have more than one unknown, x_1, x_2, x_3 .....etc. ; therefore, we will apply the command : ones (size()) to find the values of factors of each unknowns.

$y = a_0 + a_1x_1 + a_2x_2$

Example (30): Estimate the values of the factors (a_0, a_1, and a_2)

x1	0.2	0.5	0.6	1.8	1.0	1.1
x2	0.1	0.3	0.7	0.9	1.1	1.4
y	17	26	28	23	27	24

Ans.

```
MATLAB                                                        ⊟ ▣ X
File  Edit  Debug  Desktop  Window  Help
 ▯ ☞   ✂ ▶ ▮   ⟲ ⟳   ▓ ▦   ?    C:\MATLAB7\work            ▼  ...  ▣
Shortcuts  ▪ How to Add  ▪ What's New
>> x1 = [.2 .5 .6 .8 1.0 1.1]';
x2 = [.1 .3 .4 .9 1.1 1.4]';
y  = [.17 .26 .28 .23 .27 .24]';
>> X=[ones(size(x1)) x1 x2];
>> a=X\y

a =

    0.1018
    0.4844
   -0.2847

>>

Start
```

$y = 0.1018 + 0.4844x - 0.2847x^2$

Maximum error should be calculated, so finding the error can be evaluated:
MaxErr = max(abs(Y - y)) where: Y = X*a

```
MATLAB                                                        ⊟ ▣ X
File  Edit  Debug  Desktop  Window  Help
 ▯ ☞   ✂ ▶ ▮   ⟲ ⟳   ▓ ▦   ?    C:\MATLAB7\work            ▼  ...  ▣
Shortcuts  ▪ How to Add  ▪ What's New
>> x1 = [.2 .5 .6 .8 1.0 1.1]';
x2 = [.1 .3 .4 .9 1.1 1.4]';
y  = [.17 .26 .28 .23 .27 .24]';
>> X=[ones(size(x1)) x1 x2];
>> a=X\y

a =

    0.1018
    0.4844
   -0.2847

>> Y = X*a;
>> MaxErr=max(abs(Y-y))

MaxErr =

    0.0038

>>

Start
```

CHAPTER#4: Do Loops with Conditional Statement and "For" loops

This chapter will help a programmer to program his /her project in sophisticated model by using different conditional and loops statements. Also, we try to explain more commands which help us to solve our calculations by using a computer program.

Flow chart representation of the if statement

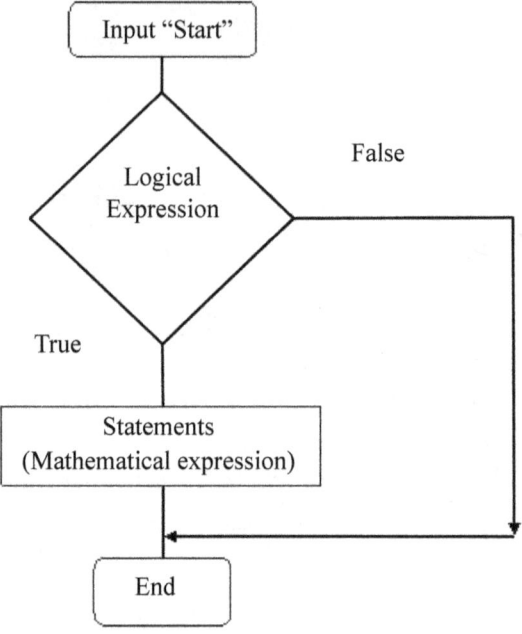

4.1. If and else Conditional Statement

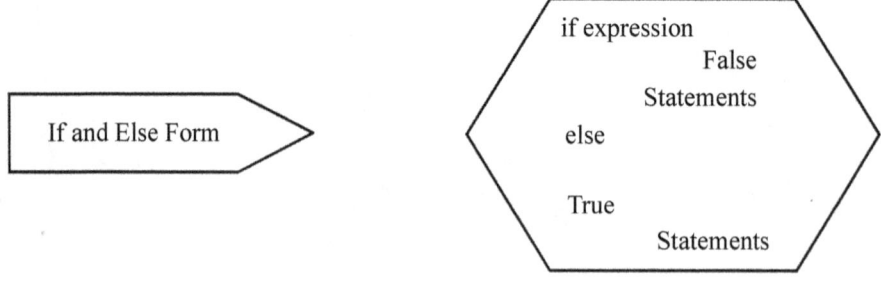

Arithmetic Layout for if statement else

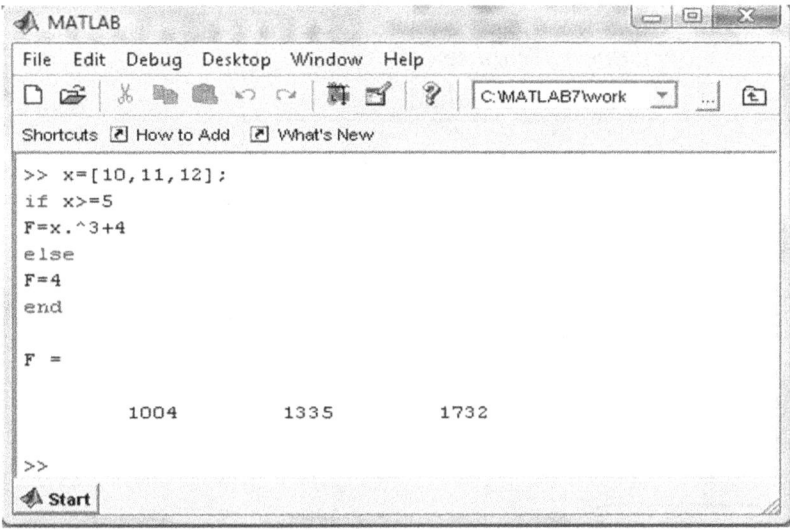

Example (31): Find the solution of F(x)

$$F(x) = \begin{cases} x^3 + 4 \\ \quad x \geq 5 \\ otherwise \\ \quad 4 \end{cases}$$

Ans.

```
>> x=[10,11,12];
if x>=5
F=x.^3+4
else
F=4
end

F =

        1004        1335        1732

>>
```

The logical operators in MATLAB

MATLAB operator	Meaning
>	greater than
<	less than
==	equal to
<=	less than or equal
>=	greater than or equal
~=	not equal to

4.1.1 Two If statements conditions

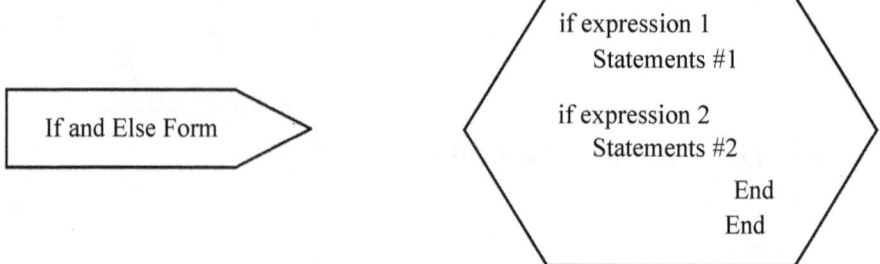

This is another form of this type of "if "conditional statement
if *logical expression 1 & logical expression 2*
Statements
end

4.2. If and else if Conditional Statement

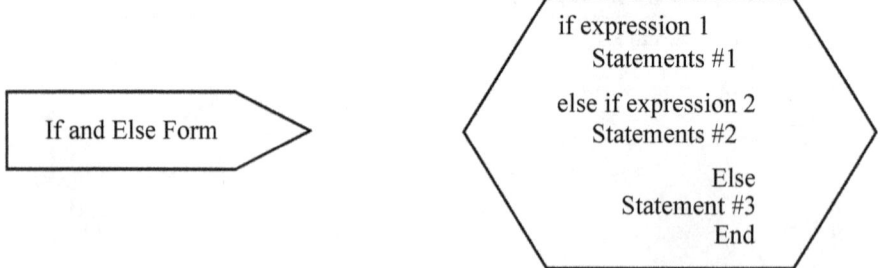

Arithmetic Layout for if statement else

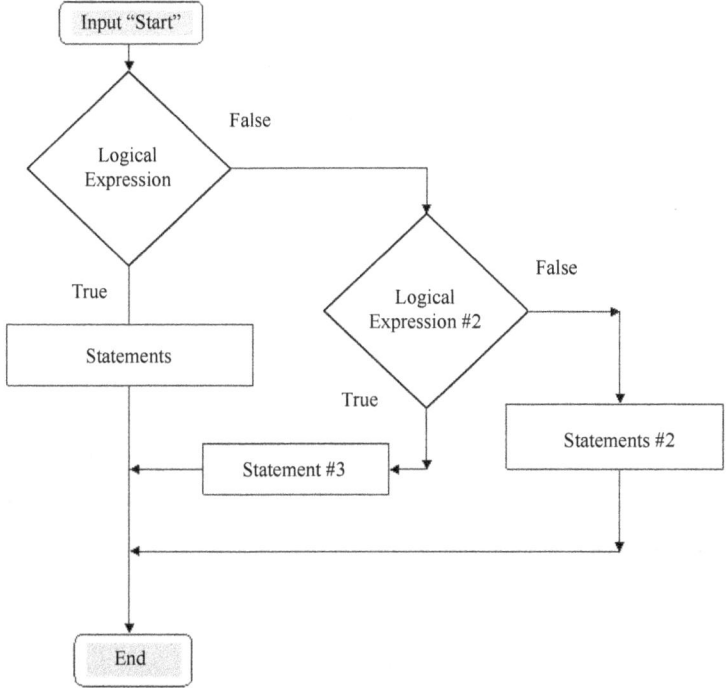

Example (32): Suppose that y = log(x) for *x* >10, *y* = sqrt(*x*) for 0 <= x <= 10, and y = exp(x) -1for x < 0. The following statements will compute y if x has already a scalar value. For k=0:1:10, and x=k^2+1

Step#1: From New M-File save as and create the program.

```
1    for k=0:1:10
2    x=k^2+1;
3            if x>100
4                 y=log(x)
5            elseif x>=0
6                 y=sqrt(x)
7            else
8                 y=exp(x)-1
9            end
10
11   end
12
```

Step#2: save and run

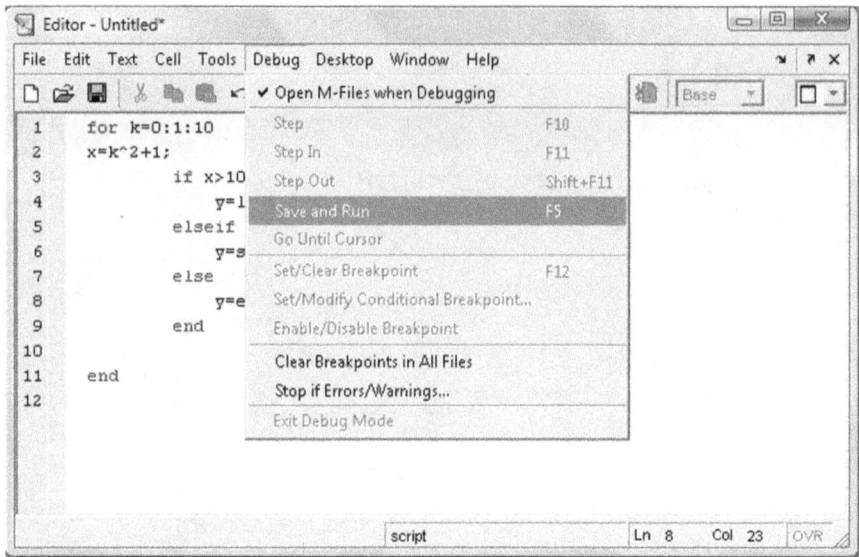

Notice: if you have already saved a program, you might press F5 to get the output of your program.

4.3. For loop Statement

The loop statement is used to trial and error. Also, it might be used to evaluate certain calculations.

Notice: the following rules when using "for loop" with the loop variable expression "k = m:i:n":

1. The step value s may be negative.

    Example: k = 10:-2:4produces k = 10, 8, 6, 4.

2. If "i"is omitted, the step value defaults to 1.

3. If" i "is positive, the loop will not be executed if "m "is greater than "n".

4. If"i "is negative, the loop will not be executed if"m" is less than "n".

5. If m equals to "i", the loop will be executed only once.

6. If the step value "i" is not an integer, round-off errors can cause the loop to execute a different number of passes than intended.

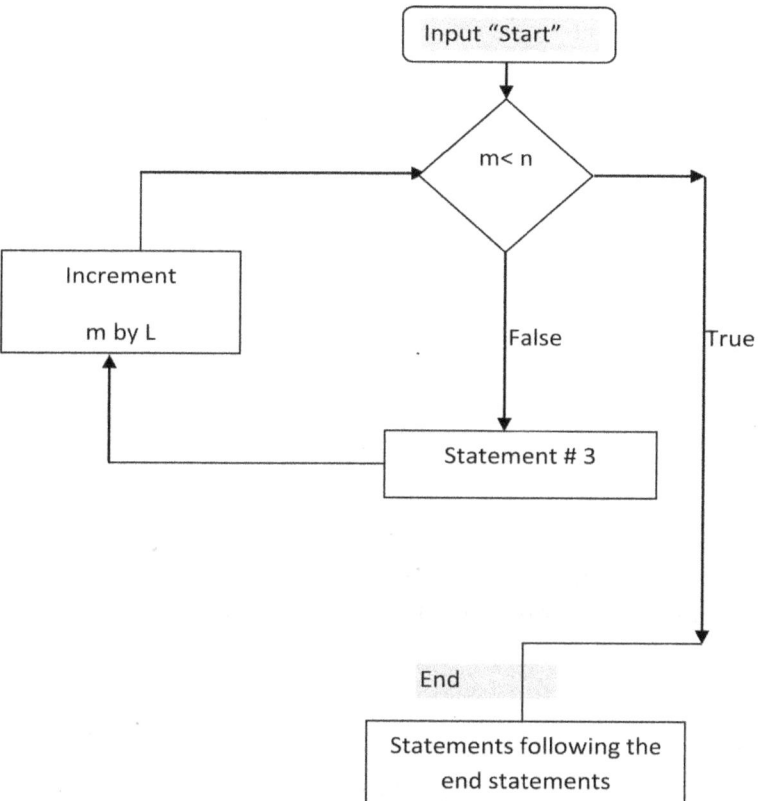

Example (33): Compute the value of this function at 5, 15, and 25 by using for loop.

$x = k^3 + k^2 + 8$

Ans.

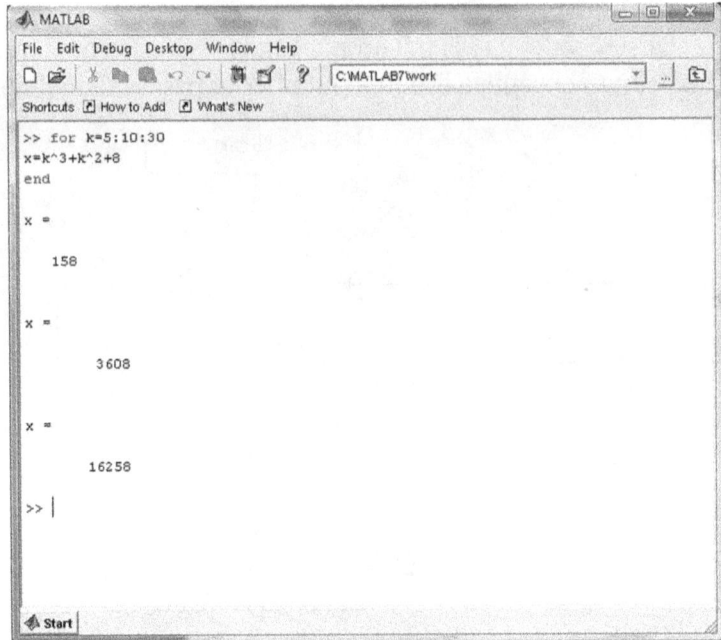

The values of x are at k = 5, k=15, and k=25 because the increment is 10. Therefore, the output of this function is three as shown.

CHAPTER #5: Digital and Signal Analysis

5.1. Eigshow and Singular Value Show

This command is used to present a graphical experiment showing the effect on the unit circle of the mapping induced by various 2-by-2 matrices. A push button allows us to choose neither "eig" mode or "svd" mode.

Command	Meaning
eigshow	Experiment show
svd	Singular value show

Notice: A matrix should have 2 rows and 2 columns.

Example (34): Use "eigshow" to show graphical effect on the unit circle for the following matrix x = [1 2 ; 4 6] and find the singular value.

Ans.

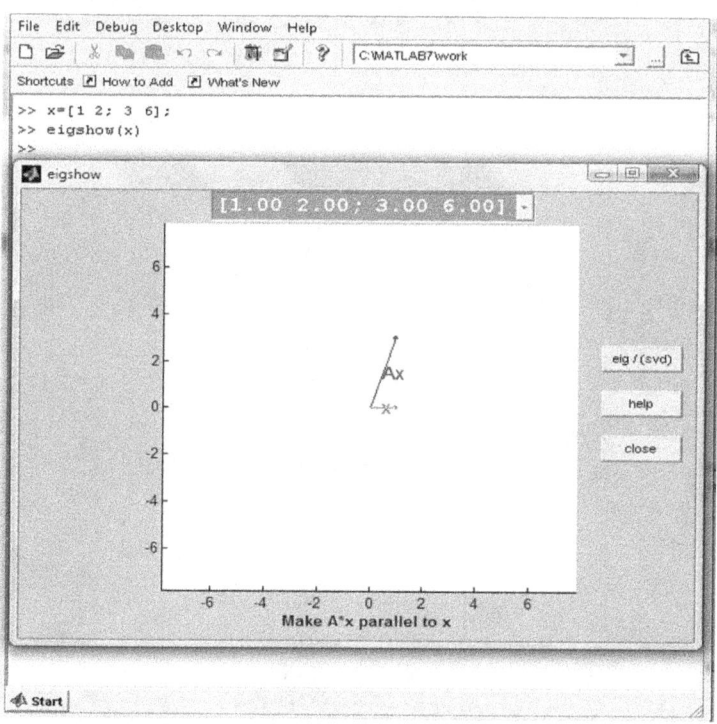

Also, you can find the "svd" by graphical as shown

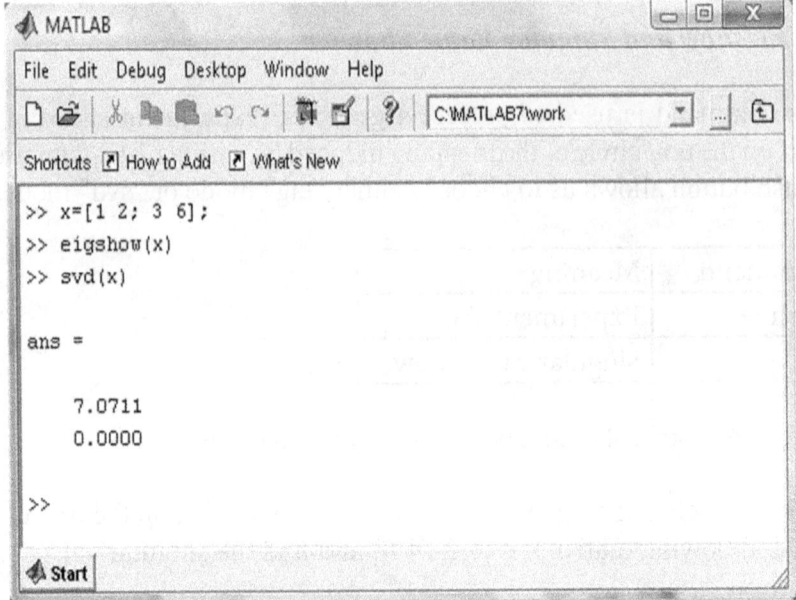

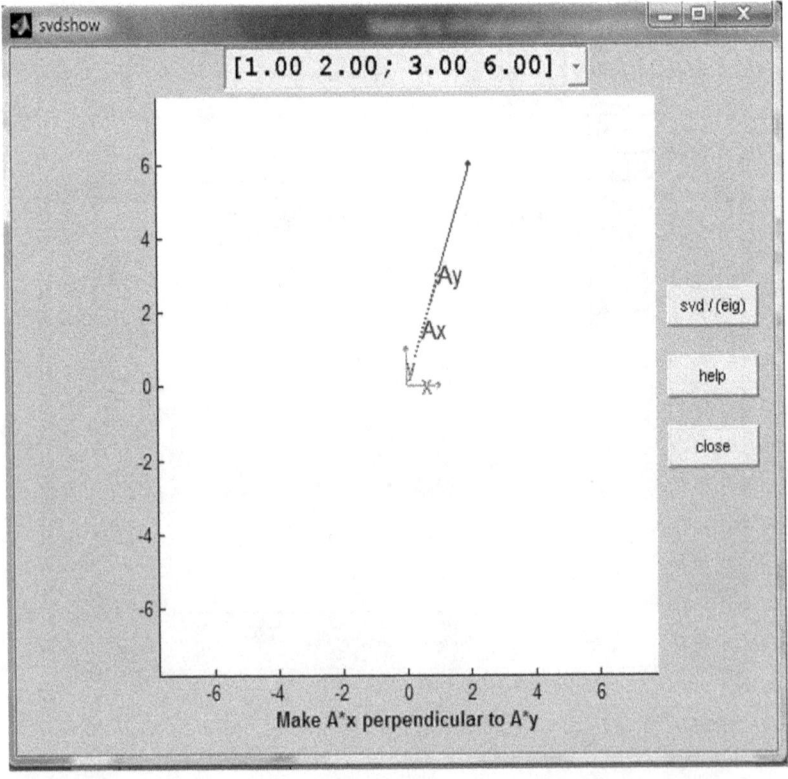

5.2. Fourier Analysis or Transform for a signal

A common use of Fourier transforms is to find the frequency components of a signal buried in a noisy time domain signal

Example (35): Consider data sampled at 2000 Hz. Form a signal containing 50 Hz and 120 Hz and corrupt it with some zero-mean random noise. The time ranges from 0.0 to 0.60, increment is 0.001, x = cos (2×pi×50×t)+cos(2×pi×120×t).

Ans.

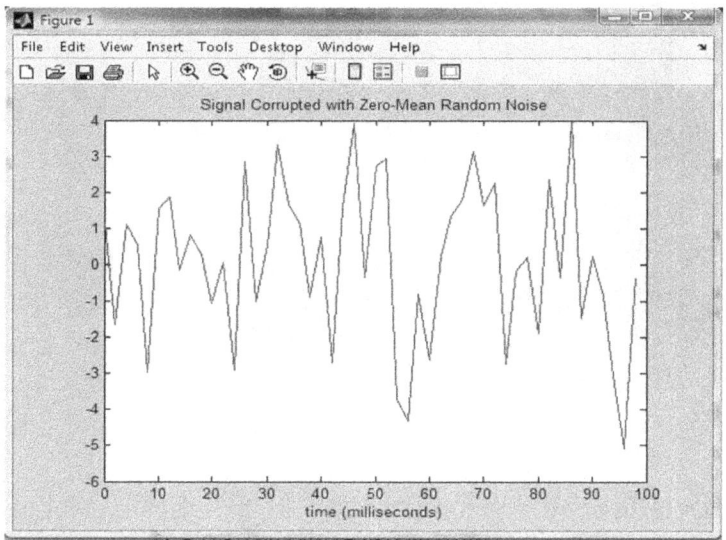

Converting to the frequency domain, the discrete Fourier transform of the noisy signal y is found by taking the 512-point fast Fourier transform FFT. Graph the first 257 points (the other 255 points are redundant) on a meaningful frequency axis.

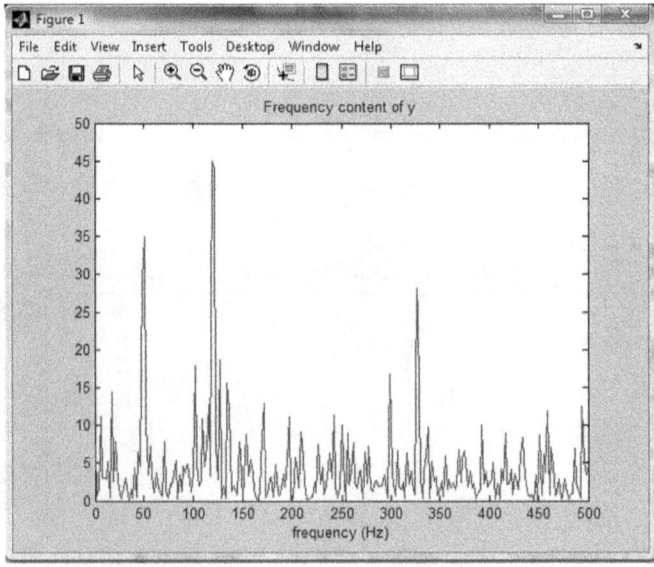

DFT

The discrete Fourier transform, or DFT, is the primary tool of digital signal processing.

FFT

Fourier Frequency transform or FFT is based on Time-Frequency.

Example (36): Find the FFT, DFT of x (t), magnitude of the vector x (t), phase and angle and also show phase and magnitude on a figure.
t= [0.0:1/25:23], x(t) = cos (2×π×25t)+ cos(2×π×40×t)

Ans.

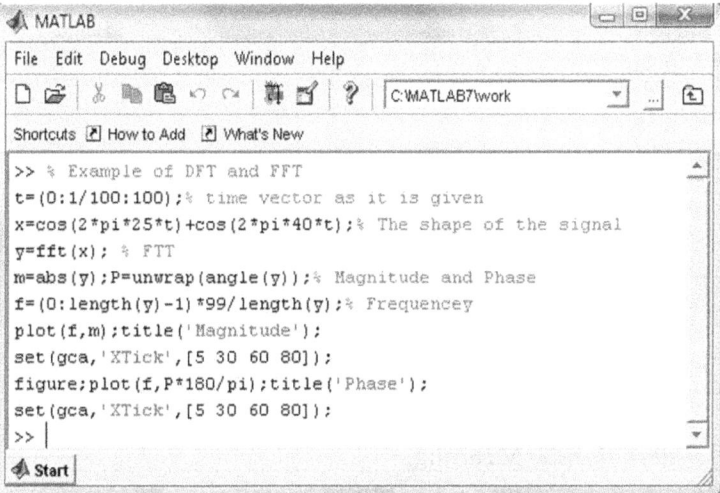

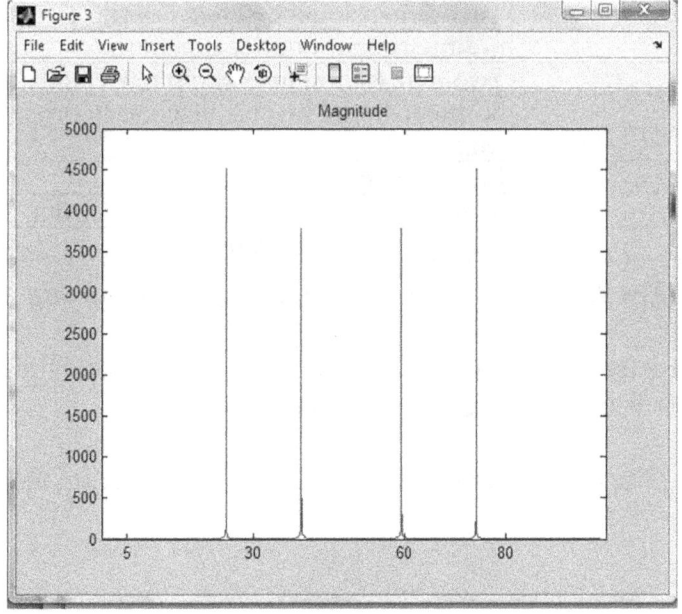

Phase Chart

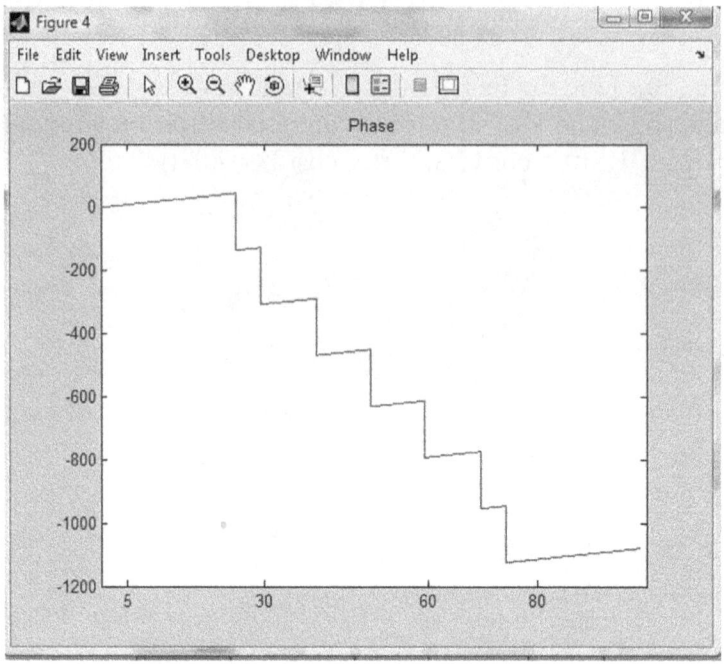

MATLAB commands	Meaning
fft	Discrete Fourier transform
ifft	Inverse discrete Fourier transform
fft2	Two-dimensional discrete Fourier transform
fftn	n-dimensional Fourier transform
ifft2	Two-dimensional inverse discrete Fourier transform
ifftn	N-dimensional inverse discrete Fourier transform
abs	Magnitude
angle	Phase angle
fftshift	Move zeroth lag to center of spectrum
unwrap	Unwrap phase angle in radians

5.3. Analysis Tool window for Frequency and Time domain

We can use (**command**: wintool) to find the frequency and time domain of a vector which has length n. A vector is rectangular.

Example (37): find the Freq. and time domain for 20 length of the vector x?

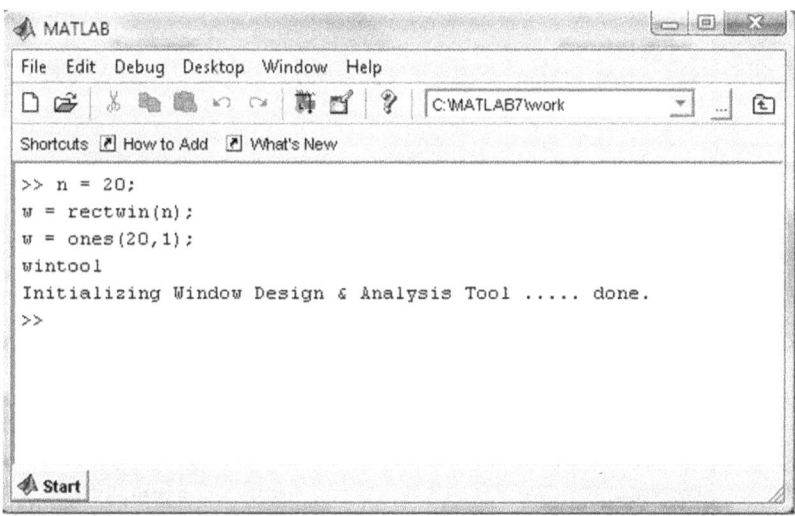

Step#1: window design & analysis tool shows up.
Step#2: if the window does not show up under the window information,
        add the window.
Step#3: Change the type of the window to rectangular.
Step#4: Change the length of a vector.

Step#1

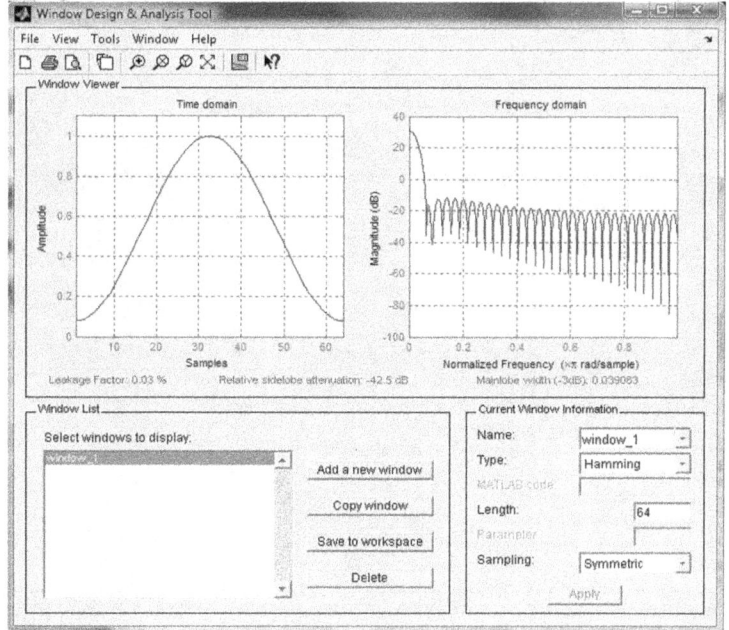

Step#2

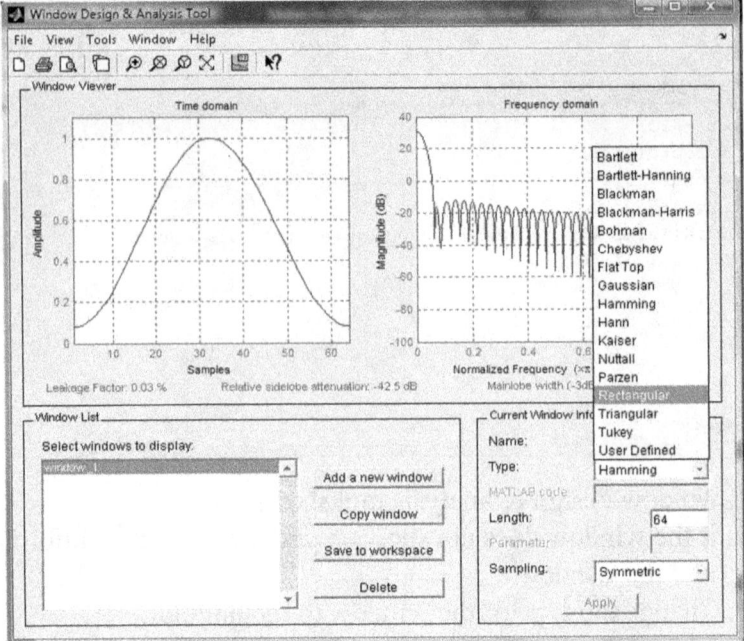

Step#4

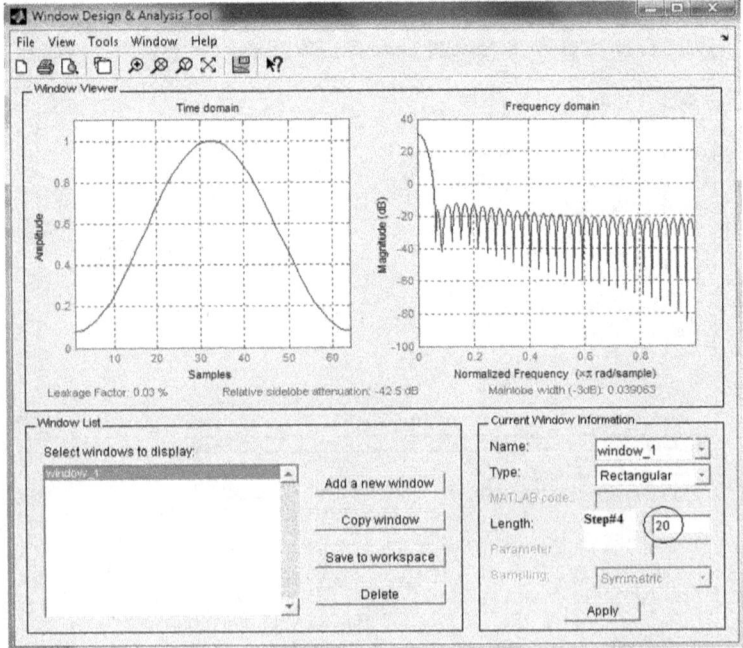

Then apply the new window information

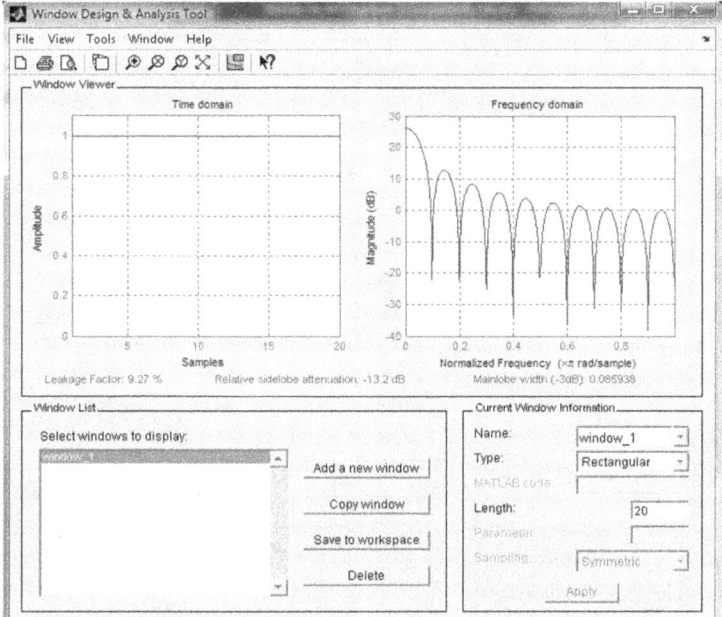

The functions (bartlett) and (triang) compute similar triangular windows, with three important differences. The Bartlett function always returns a window with two zeros on the ends of the sequence, so that for "n" odd, the center section of Bartlett (n+2) is equivalent to triang(n)

The bartlett function shape "by changing the type of window"

The triangle function shape" by changing the type of window"

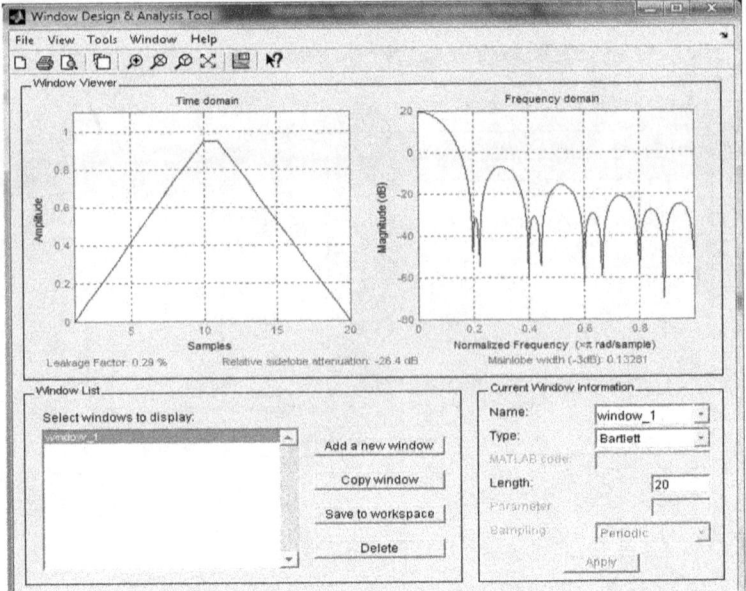

The triangle function ahape" by changing the type of window"

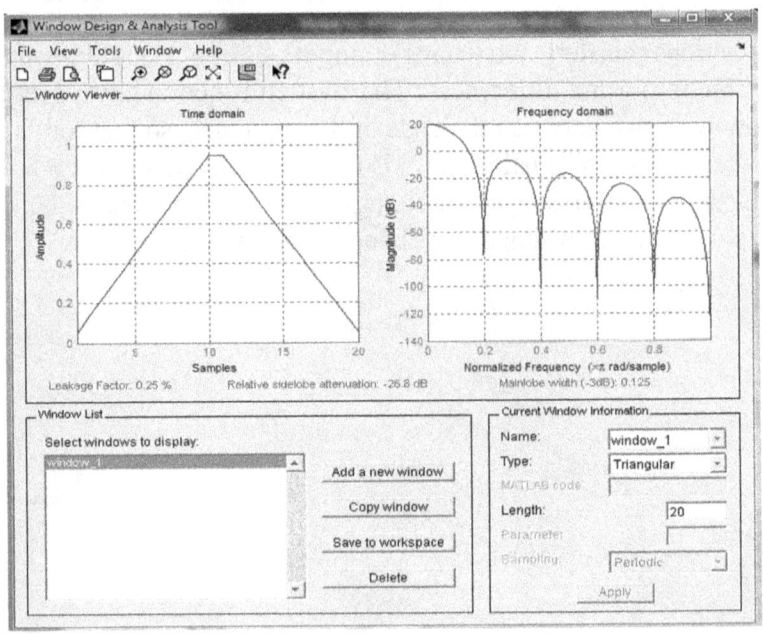

5.4. Signal Analysis by using two commands: firls and firpm

The functions of "firls" and "firpm" are used to filtrate the linear phase. To compare their frequency responses using FV Tool (Filter visualization tool).

Example (38): A low pass example with approximate amplitude 1 from 0 to 0.4 Hz, and approximate amplitude 0 from 0.5 to 1.0 Hz. The filtrating of the frequency phase can be done using "fvtool? For n=30 filter order?

Ans.

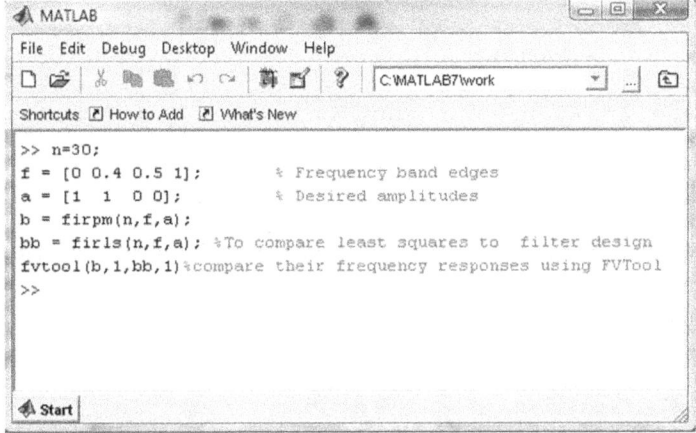

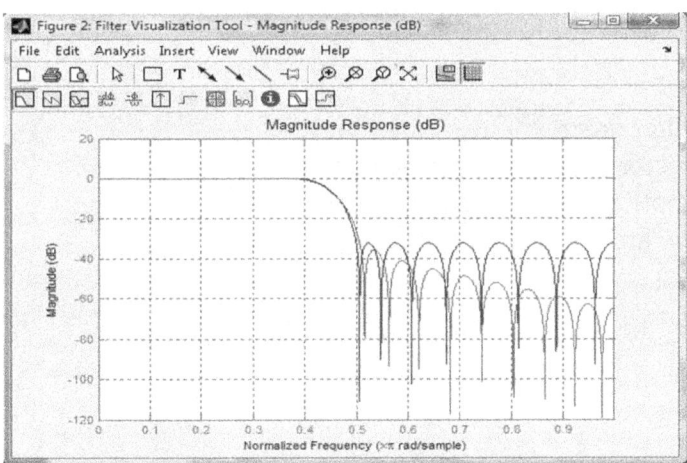

Notice: you can change the magnitude response by using analysis icon. Change analysis window

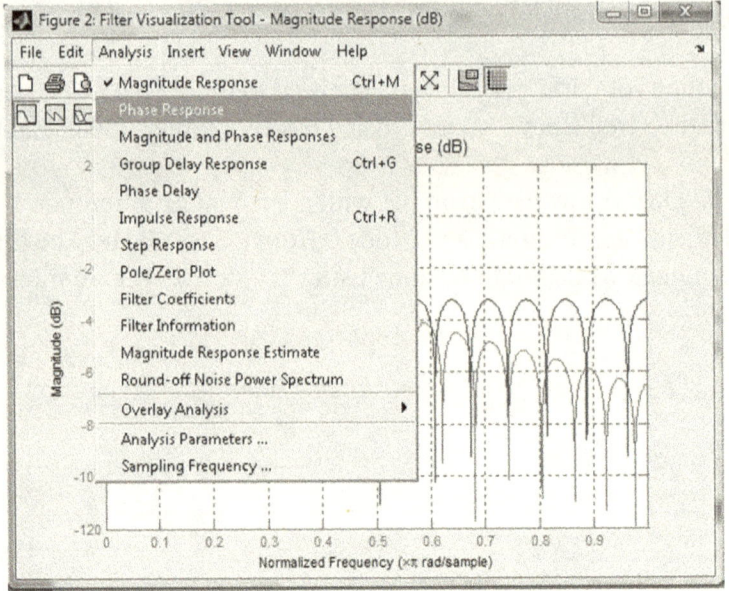

5.5. Complex FIR Filter Design with Transition Bands (command: cfirpm)

The command of "cfirpm" allows arbitrary frequency-domain constraints to be specified for the design of a possibly complex FIR filter

Example (39): Design a 31-tap, linear-phase, low pass filter, and design a nonlinear-phase all pass FIR filter: if the filter order is 30.

Where:
n is the filter order
f is the vector of frequency band edges.
p_1, p_2 are optional parameters that may be passed to fresp.
dh and dw are the desired complex frequency.

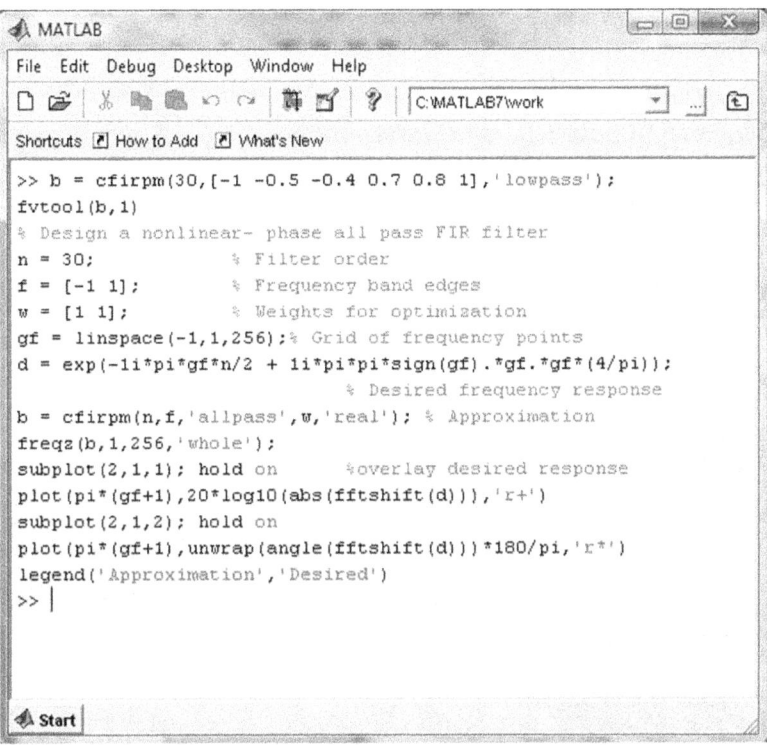

```
>> b = cfirpm(30,[-1 -0.5 -0.4 0.7 0.8 1],'lowpass');
fvtool(b,1)
% Design a nonlinear- phase all pass FIR filter
n = 30;              % Filter order
f = [-1 1];          % Frequency band edges
w = [1 1];           % Weights for optimization
gf = linspace(-1,1,256);% Grid of frequency points
d = exp(-1i*pi*gf*n/2 + 1i*pi*pi*sign(gf).*gf.*gf*(4/pi));
                     % Desired frequency response
b = cfirpm(n,f,'allpass',w,'real'); % Approximation
freqz(b,1,256,'whole');
subplot(2,1,1); hold on        %overlay desired response
plot(pi*(gf+1),20*log10(abs(fftshift(d))),'r+')
subplot(2,1,2); hold on
plot(pi*(gf+1),unwrap(angle(fftshift(d)))*180/pi,'r*')
legend('Approximation','Desired')
>> |
```

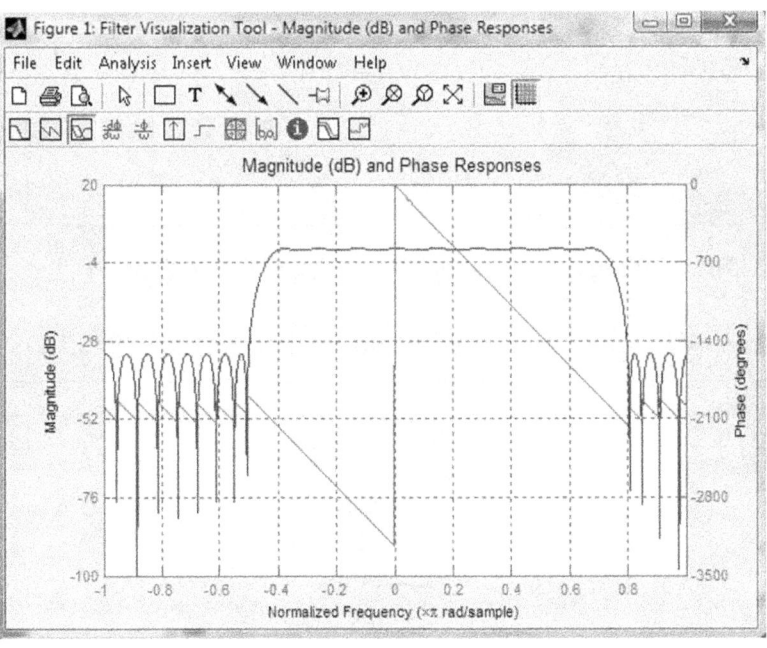

CHAPTER #6:   *Variety Topics*

6.1. One and two-dimensional interpolations

6.1.1. One dimensional interpolation (command: interp1)

The interp1 command is a MATLAB M-file. The 'nearest' and 'linear' methods have straightforward applications.

Example (40): Find the value of temperature at 175 kPa for the following values values P = 100, 150, 160, 170, 180 and 200 if T= 100, 111, 128, 130, 135,179 C.

Ans.

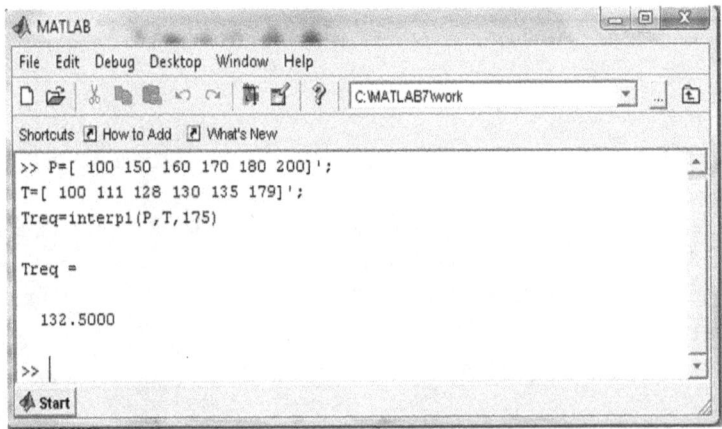

6..1.2. Two- dimensional interpolation (command: interp1)

Example (41): Given this set of employee data, years = 1950:10:1990;

service	10,20,30
Salary	170, 200.592, 187.625, 179.323,195.072, 250.287, 203.212,179.092, 322.767 226.505,153.706, 426.730, 249.633, 120.281, 549

Find the wage earned in 1965 by an employee with 17 years' service?

Ans.

```
MATLAB
File  Edit  Debug  Desktop  Window  Help
D ☞ ┃ ✕ ▶ ▦ ▫ ∽ ⌐ ┃ 賦 ◙ ┃ ? ┃ C:\MATLAB7\work                                    ▼ ┃ .. ┃ 🖹
Shortcuts ▣ How to Add ▣ What's New

>> % finding the wage earned in 1965 by an employee with 17 years' service by using interp2
years = 1950:10:1990;
service = 10:10:30;
salary = [170.34 200.592 187.625
          179.323 195.072 250.287
          203.212 179.092 322.767
          226.505 153.706 426.730
          249.633 120.281 549];
Salary = interp2(service,years,salary,17,1965)% Salary at 1965 with 17 years' service

Salary =

  188.3377

>>
```

6.2. Finite Elements Using MATLAB command

The "PDE" is a tool which stands for Partial Differential Equation. This tool is used to help a programmer solving a problem numerically using finite element method. To invite this command, we should write "pdetool" command in the command window.

Step#1: calling-up the "pdetool "command

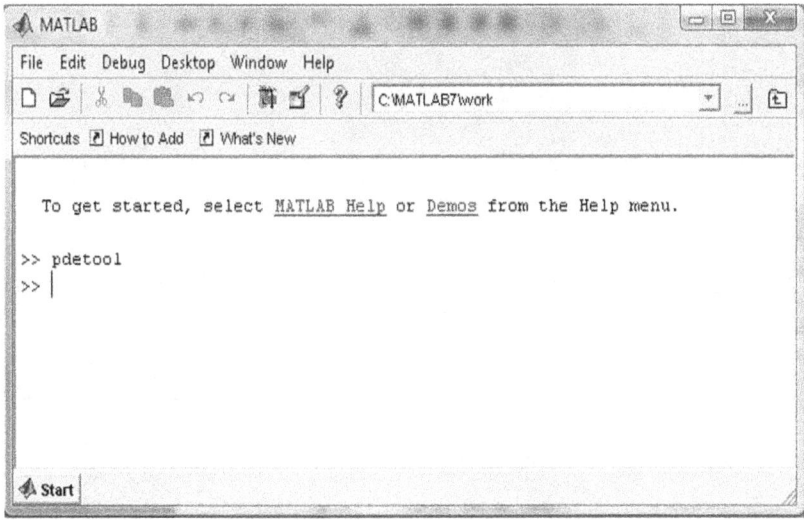

*Step#2: th*e new window will show up similar to this window

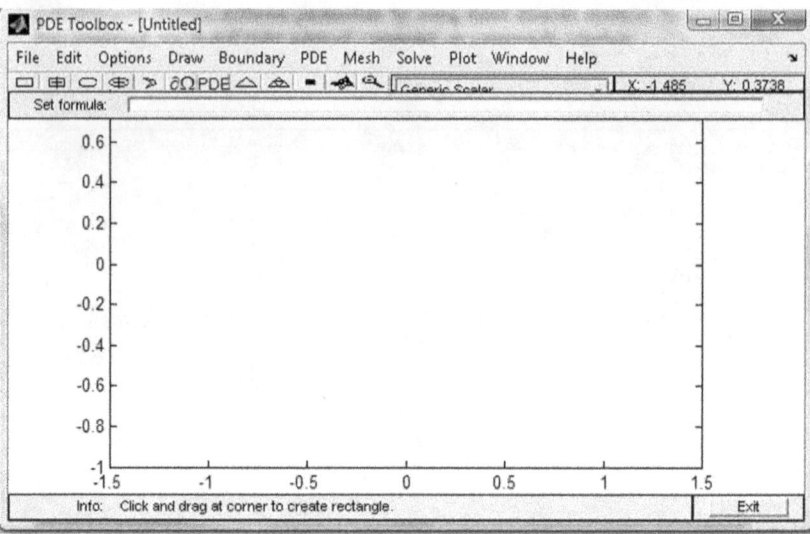

Step#3: Draw the shape (square + circle)

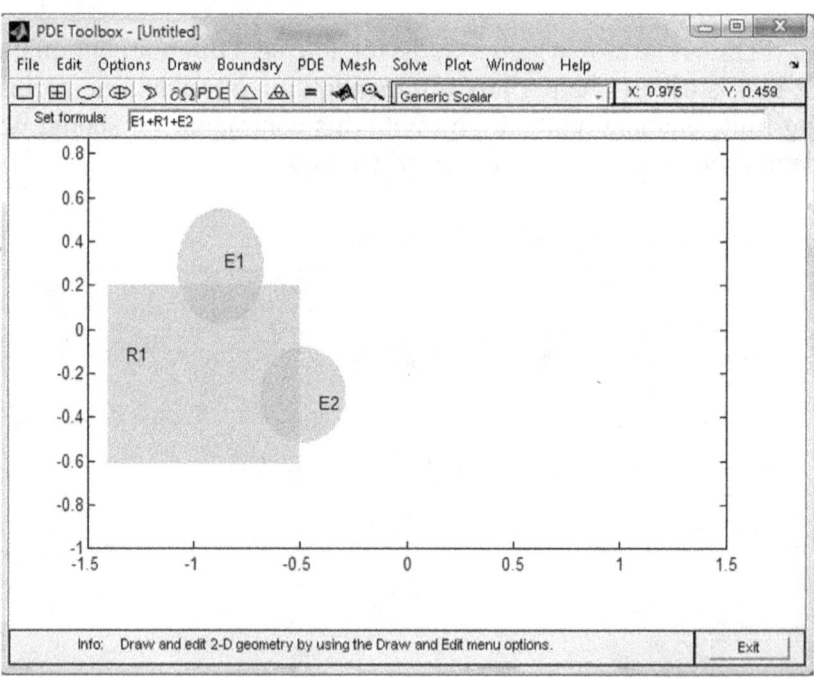

Step#4: Save as your model from File + save as

Step#5: Enter the boundary mode of the model by clicking the icon δΩ or by selecting boundary mode from the Boundary menu

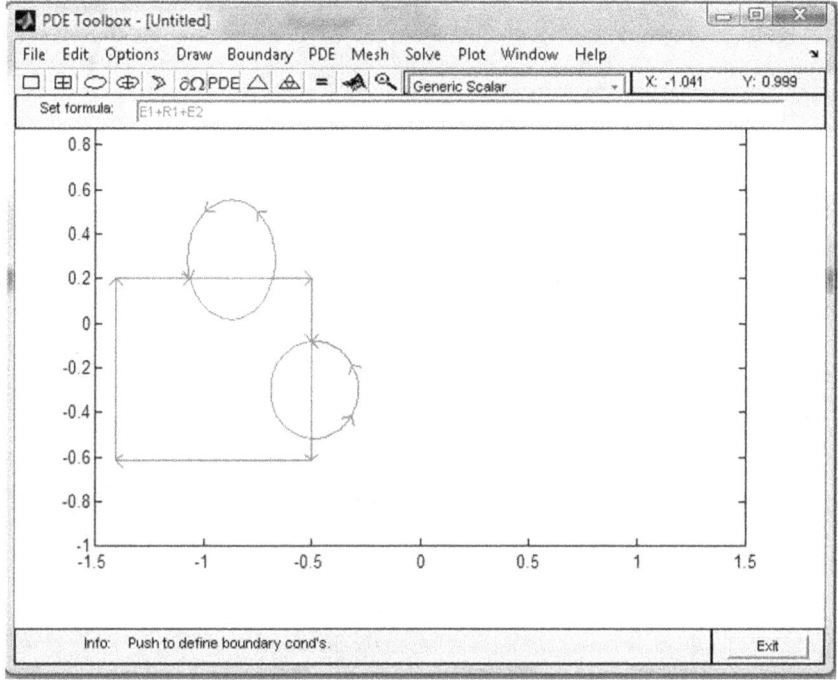

Step#6: Double-clicking anywhere on the selected boundary segments and it opens the boundary condition dialog box

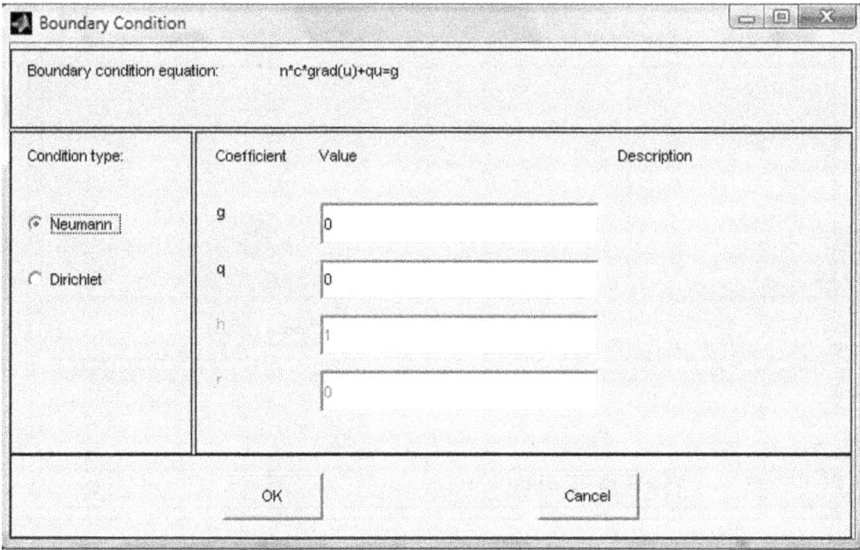

Step #7: Select the value for g parameter, then press OK.

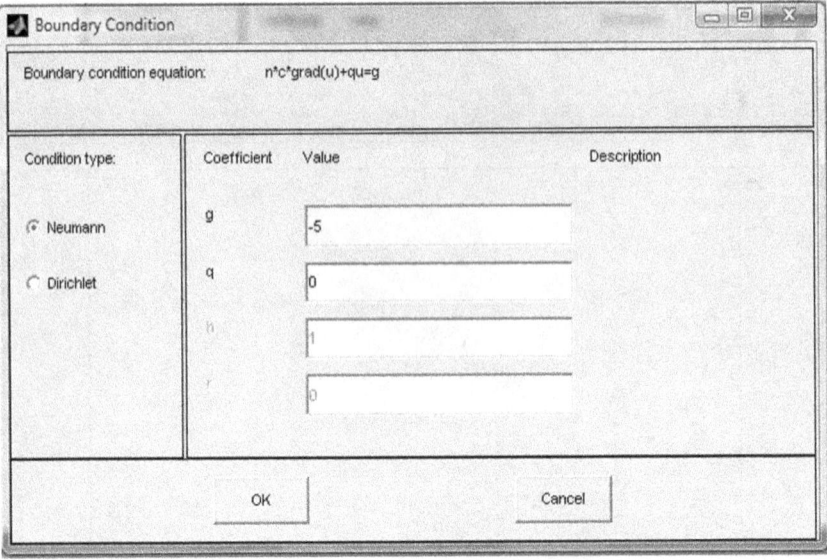

Step#8: Press on PDE icon

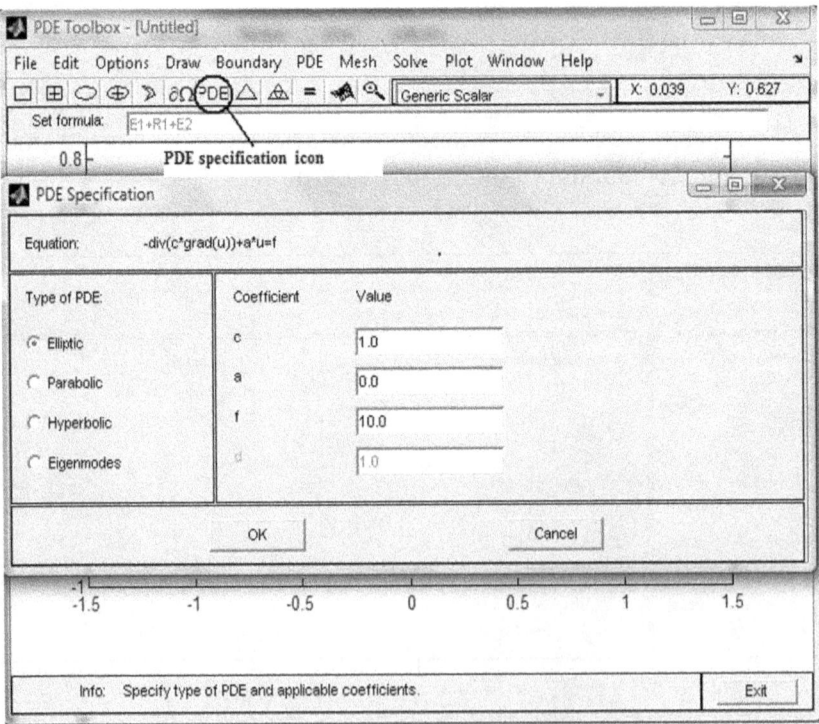

Step#9: Finally, create the square mesh that the PDE Tool box uses in the Finite Element Method (FEM) to solve the PDE

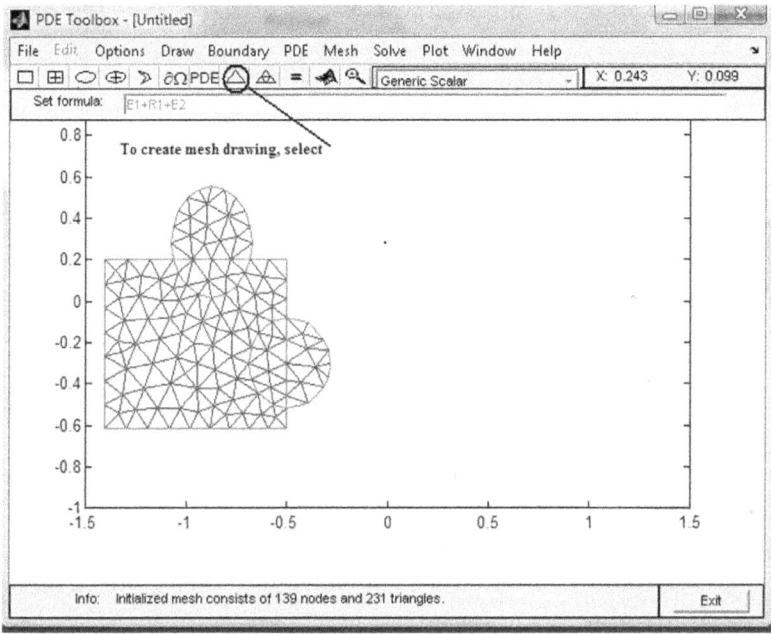

Solve PDE by clicking on Solve icon.

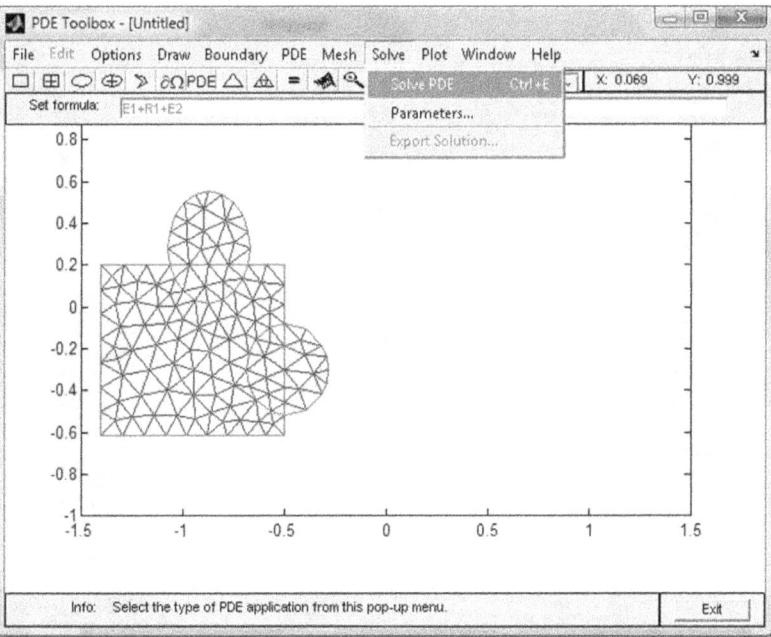

Final step: the solution

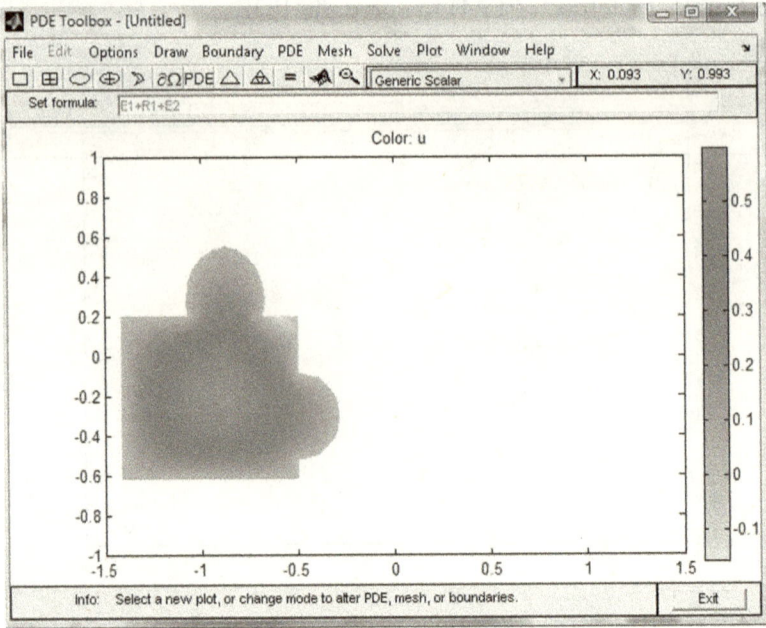

To change the plot, go to the plot icon and select parameter and then change the plot and the color of the plot if you want e.g. 3D-height. Then click plot and done.

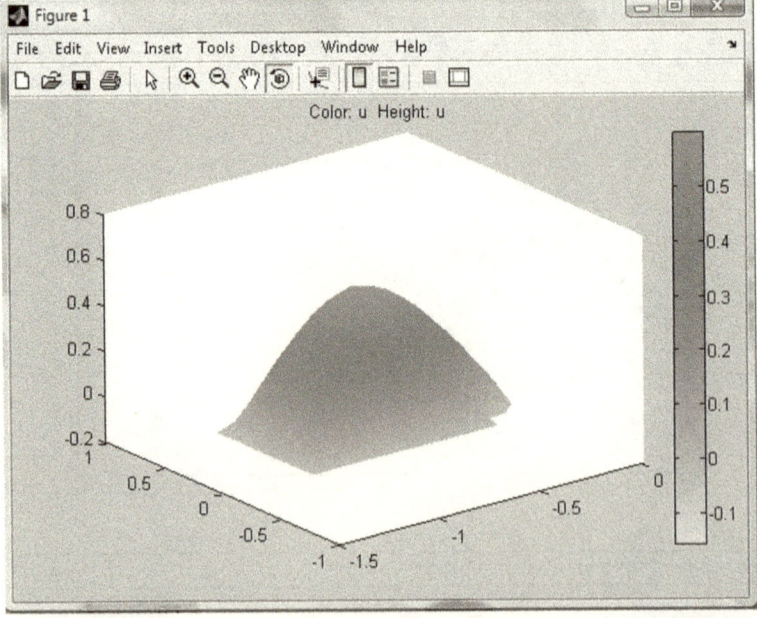

6.3. Finite Elements Applications Using MATLAB Commands

6.3.1. Heat Distribution in Radioactive Rod

Example (42): Solve this problem using the pdetool GUI. Model the rod as a rectangle with its base along the x-axis, and let the x-axis be the z direction and the y-axis be the r direction. A rectangle with corners in (-1.5,0), (1.5,0), (1.5,0.2), and (-1.5,0.2) would then model a rod with length 3 and radius 0.2. Enter the boundary conditions by double-clicking the boundaries to open the Boundary Condition dialog box. For the left end, use Neumann conditions with 0 for q and 5000×y for g. For the right end, use Dirichlet conditions with 1 for h and 100 for r. For the outer boundary, use Neumann conditions with 50×y for q and 50×y×100 for g. For the axis, use Neumann conditions with 0 for q and g. Enter the coefficients into the PDE Specification dialog box: c is 40×y, a is zero, d is 7800×500×y, and f is 20000×y. Animate the solution over a span of 20000 seconds (computing the solution every 1000 seconds). We can see how heat flows in over the right and outer boundaries as long as u < 100, and out when u > 100. You can also open the PDE Specification dialog box, and change the PDE type to Elliptic. This shows the solution when u does not depend on time, i.e., the steady state solution. The profound effect of cooling on the outer boundary can be demonstrated by setting the heat transfer coefficient to zero. (This example has been mentioned in MATLAB version 7)

The final answer will be

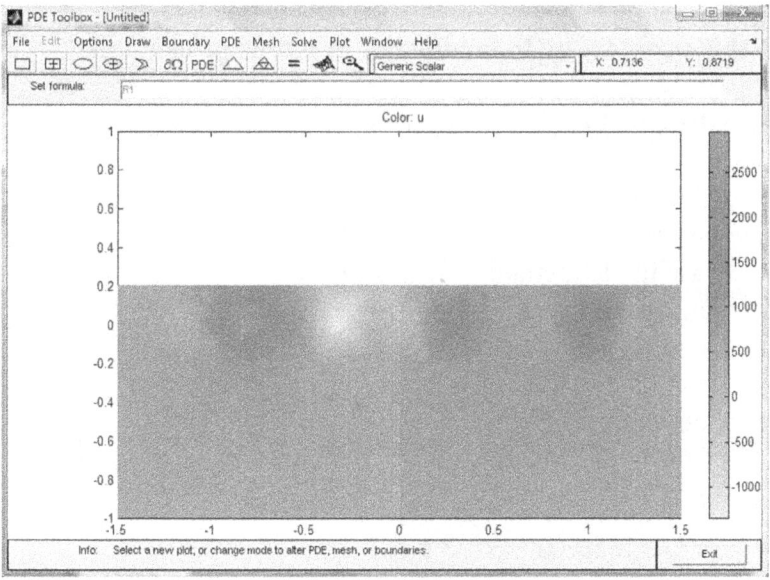

Example (43): Consider a steel plate that is clamped along a right-angle inset at the lower left corner, and pulled along a rounded cut at the upper right corner. All other sides are free. The steel plate has the following properties: Dimension: 1-by-1 meters; thickness 1mm; inset is 1/4-by-1/4 meters. The rounded cut runs from (2/4, 1) to (1, 2/4). Young's modulus: 196×10^3 (MN/m^2), Poisson's ratio: 0.31. The curved boundary is subjected to an outward normal load of 500 N/m. We need to specify a surface traction; we therefore divide by the thickness 1 mm, thus the surface tractions should be set to 0.5 MN/m^2. We will use the force unit MN in this example. We want to compute a number of interesting quantities, such as the x- and y-direction strains and stresses, the shear stress, and the von Mises effective stress.

Problem Analysis

Using the pdetool command, the first thing to do is to select the application mode. For this problem, use **Structural Mechanics, Plane Stress**. The CSG model can be made very quickly by drawing a polygon with corners in x=[0 2/4 1 1 1/4 1/4 0] and y=[1 1 2/4 0 0 1/4 1/4] and a circle with center in x=2/4, y=2/4 and radius 1/4

The rounded cut is subject to a Neumann condition with q=0 and g_1=0.5×nx, g_2=0.5×ny. The remaining boundaries are free (no normal stress), that is, a Neumann condition with q=0 and g=0 (similar to this problem has been mentioned in MATLAB program version 7)

Solve this problem by following the pervious procedures.

6.4. Creating MATLAB Animations

MATLAB allows users to use three ways of generating moving and animated graphics.
   a. Erase mode method.
   b. Generating movie.
   c. Using AVI files.

Erase Mode Method (EMM)

Animated figure

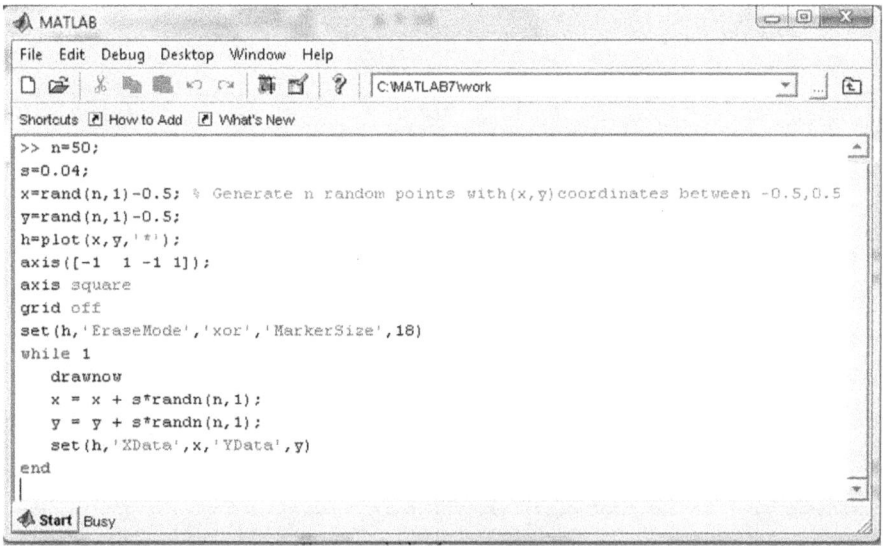

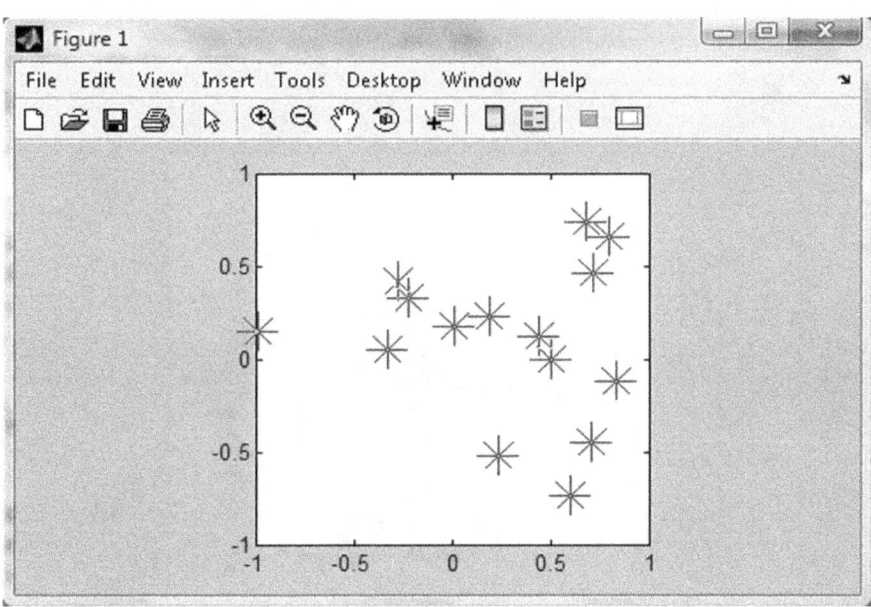

```
>> n=400; s=0.04;
>> nframes = 50;% you should decide on the number of frames
>> x = rand(n,1)-0.5;
y = rand(n,1)-0.5;
h = plot(x,y,'.');
set(h,'MarkerSize',18);
axis([-1 1 -1 1])
axis square
grid off
>> for k = 1:nframes
   x = x + s*randn(n,1);
   y = y + s*randn(n,1);        % Generate the movie and use getframe to capture each frame
   set(h,'XData',x,'YData',y)
   M(k) = getframe;
end
>> movie(M,30) % Finally, play the movie 30 times
```

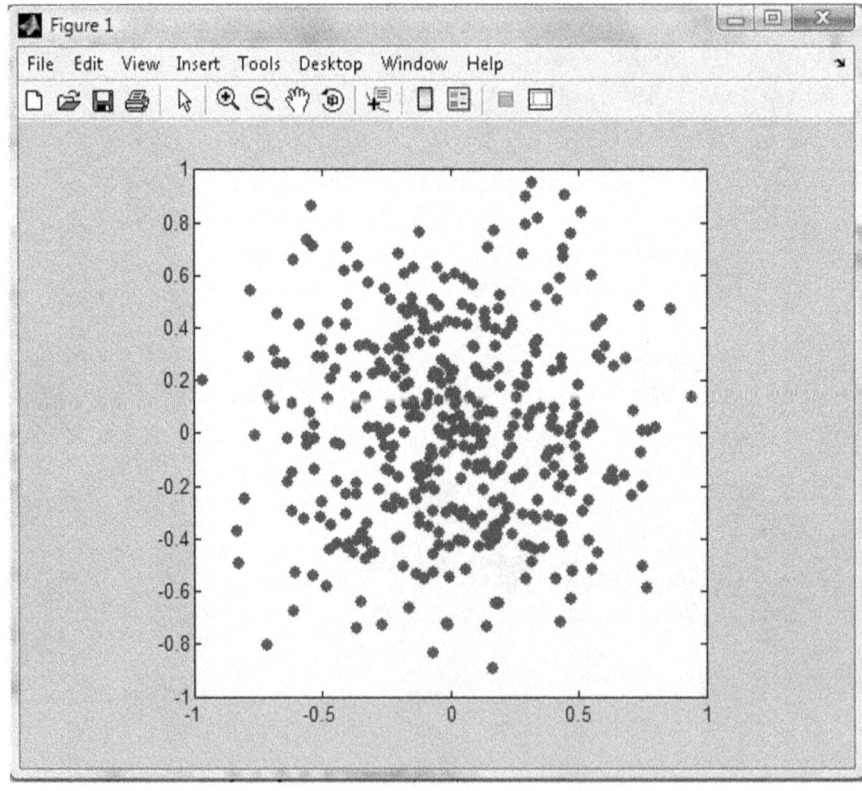

6.5. Integration and differential Functions

6.5.a. Integration functions

We can find the integration by using "int" command. In the meantime, we must define the parameters by using "syms".

Example (44): Find the following integrations
1. $\int (x + c)\, dx$
2. $\int x^n\, dx$
3. $\int (\ln(x) + xx^2)dx$
4. $\int (ax + b)\, dx$

Ans.

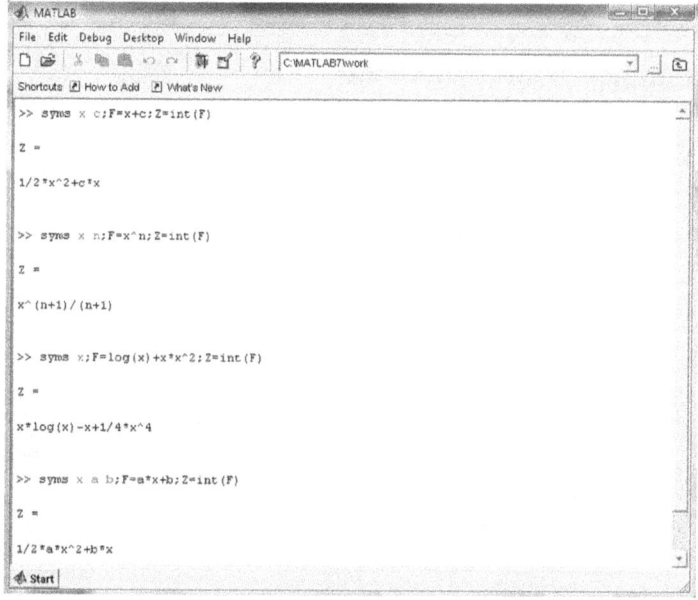

6.5.b. Plot of integration Function
The "ezplot"command is used to plot and draw the integration functions

Example (45): find the following integration function

1. $\int \left(e^{-\frac{1}{2}x} + 2x \right) dx$
2. $\int [\sin(x) \times \cos(x)]\, dx$

Ans.

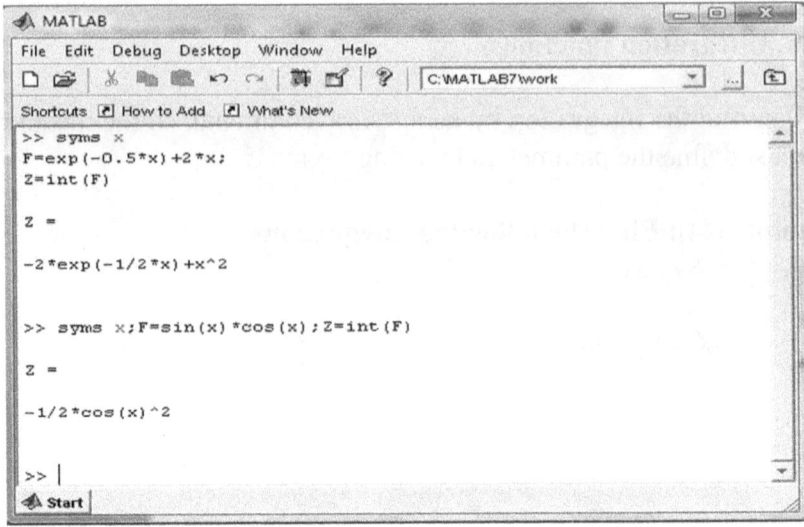

6.5.2a.. Limited integrations

We use the same "int" command to find limited integrations.

Example (46): Find the following integrations

1. $\int^b (x^3 + x^2 + 3x)\, dx$
2. $\int^2 (x + 2)\, dx$

Ans.

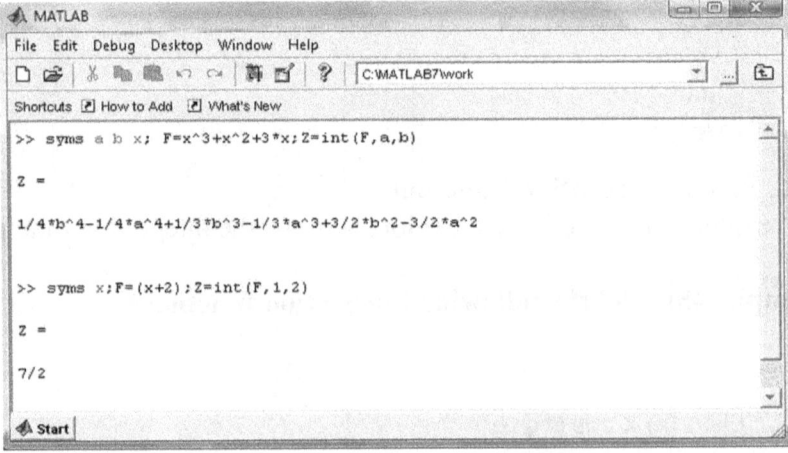

6.5.3. Differential Functions

6.5.3a Single Differential Equation

The command dsolve determines symbolic solutions to ordinary differential equations. The functions are specified by symbolic expressions containing the letter D to denote the differentiation.

Example (47): Find the following differential functions:
1. $F = x + 3$
2. $F = x^4 + x^3 + 5$

Ans.

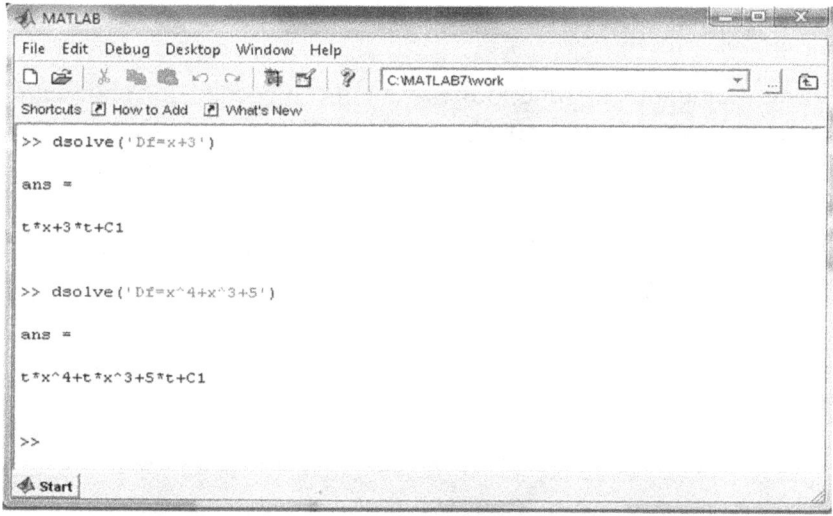

6.5.3b. Several Differential Equations

The command" dsolve" can also handle several ordinary differential equations in several variables, with or without initial conditions. For example, here is a pair of linear, first-order equations.

Example (48): Find the following differential equations

1. $F = 3x + 4y$
2. $F = -4x + 3g$

Ans.

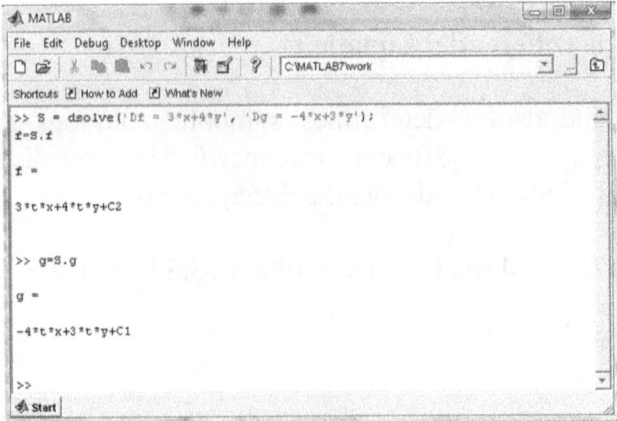

6.6. Plotting Mathematical Functions

Plotting mathematical functions is very an important for engineers or students who study in a college of science. The fplot command plots a mathematical function.

Example (49): plot the following functions for this axes limits[-5 5]
1. $F(x)= x^2 + x + 1$
2. $F(x)= x^3 + x + 5$

Ans.
1.

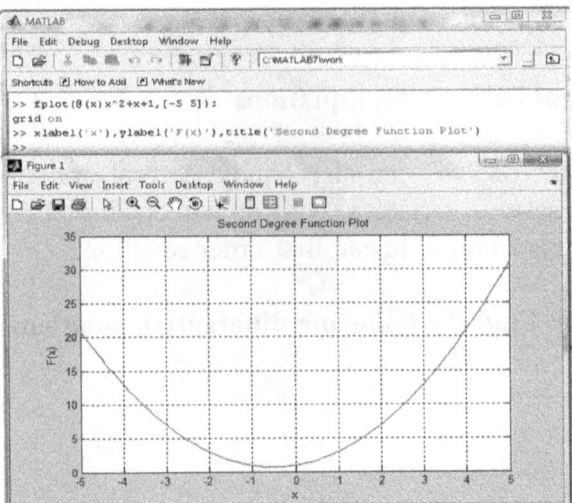

2.

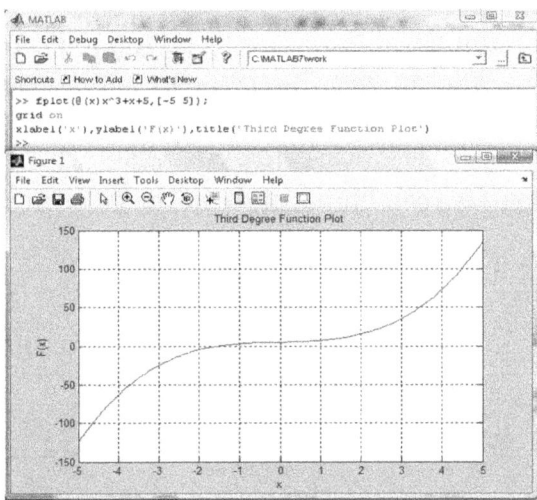

6.6.1. Plotting with Two Y-Axes

By using plotyy command, MATLAB allows us to plot two Y-axes as shown in example(50).

Example (50): plot the following function

$$F(x) = \sin(x) + 2$$

Ans.

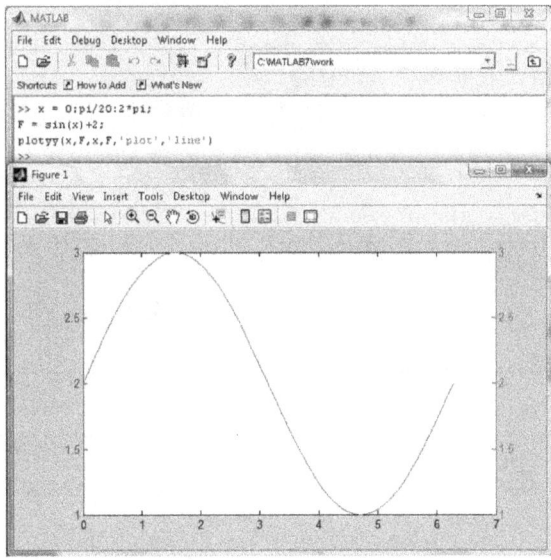

6.6.2. Combining Stem Plots with Line Plots

To combine the two types of plots can be done suing "hold on "command. To name each curve can be done using "legend" command. Plotting more than one figure windows can be done by using (figure(1),figure(2)…ets)

Example (51): plot the combining plots for the following two functions

F(x) = sin(x) + 2, F(x) = tan(x) + cos(x)

Ans.

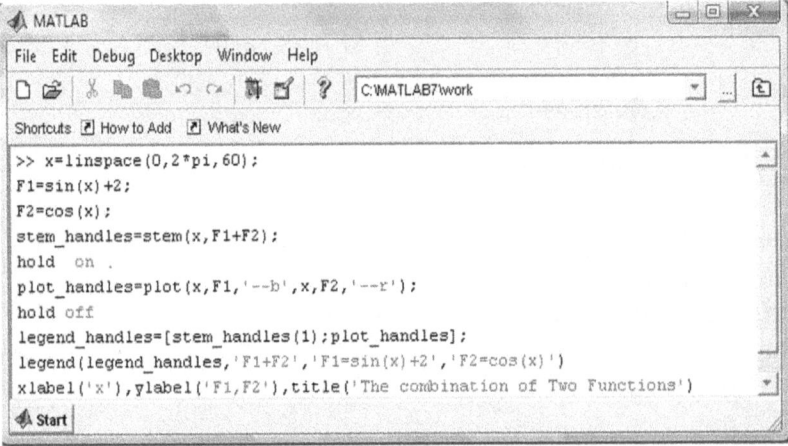

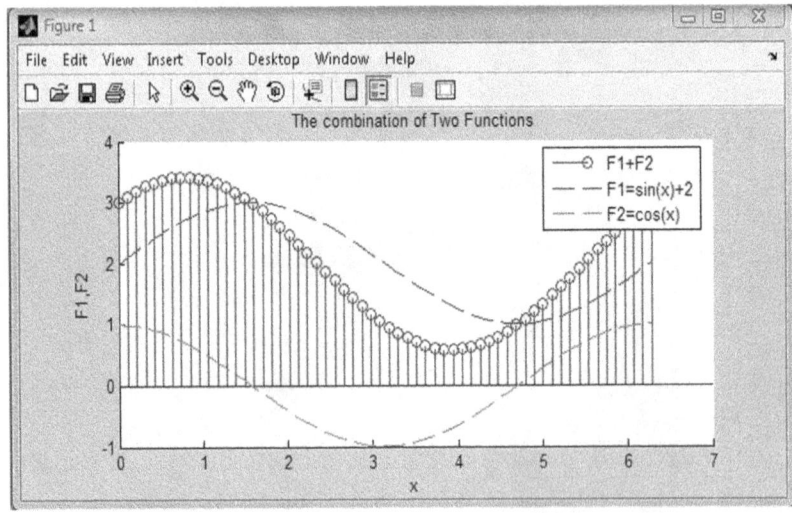

6.7. Design of Compensators (Electro hydraulic Servomechanism)

To design an electro hydraulic servo mechanisms use the MATLAB commands which enable us to design this type of mechanism. The two commands are "Gservo "and "sisotool".

Step#1: Call the commands ("Gservo" and "sisotool"). Write the two commands in command window or M-file window.

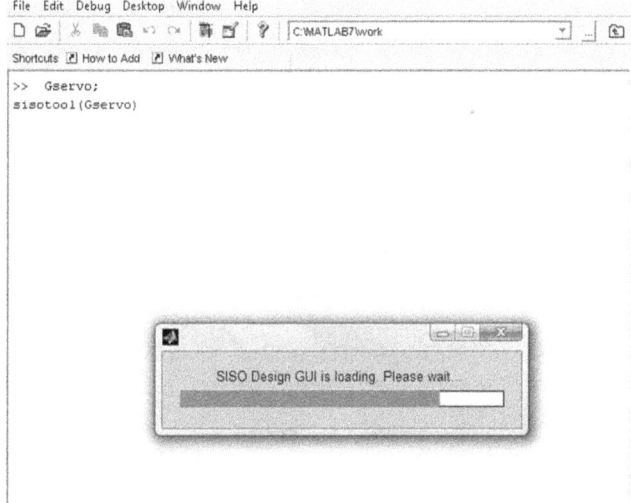

Step #2: SISO Design window.

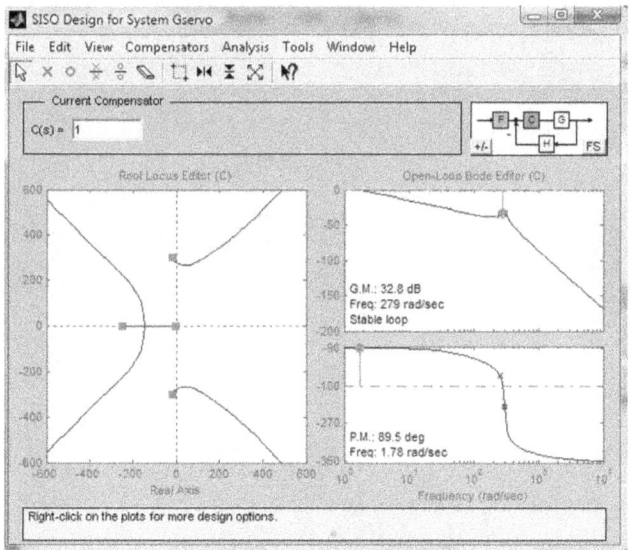

Step#3: Using of "zooming tools"

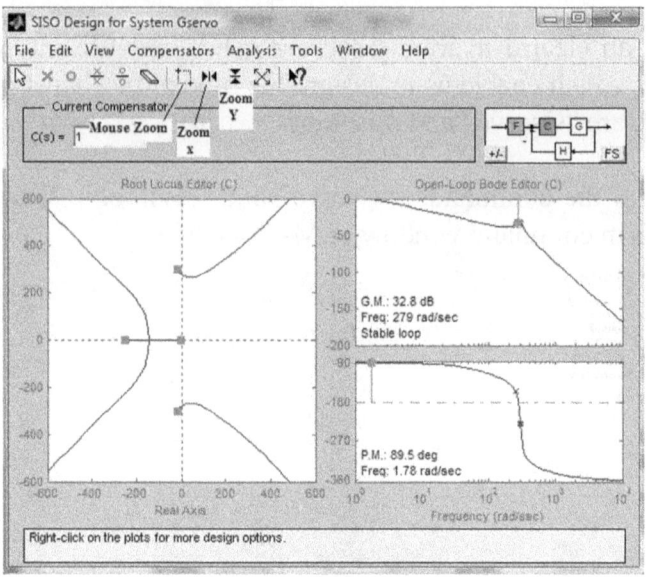

Step#4: Adding pole/zero, delete pole, and design Constrains.
Adding, deleting or design constrains are by right click on the SISO design window.

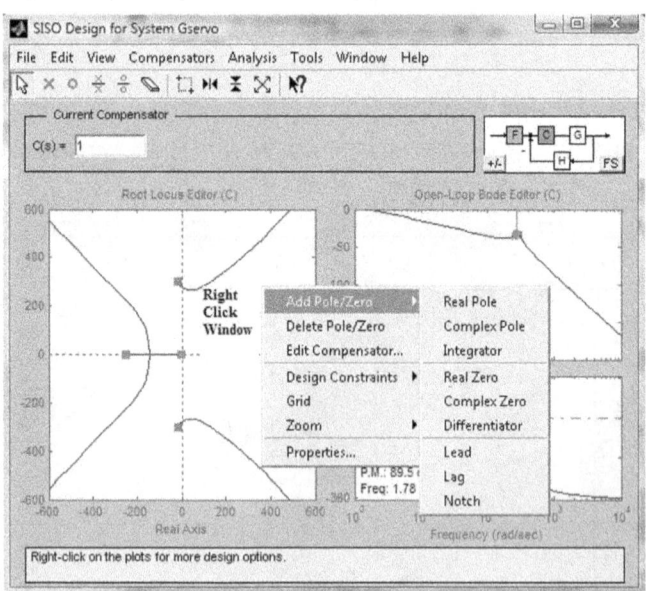

Notice: You might use this window to zoom in X, Y, or X-Y zooms.

Example (52): Design a controller to meet all the following specification The 2% settling time is less than 0.08 second. The maximum overshoot is less than 8%. Damping Ratio is 0.5 and Natural Frequency at least 1.

Ans.
1. Right click on the SISO window.
2. Select design constraints.
3. Select New.
4. Select the type of constraint.

There are four types of constraints as following
a. setting time
b. damping ratio
c. at least or at most natural frequency.
d. overshoot.

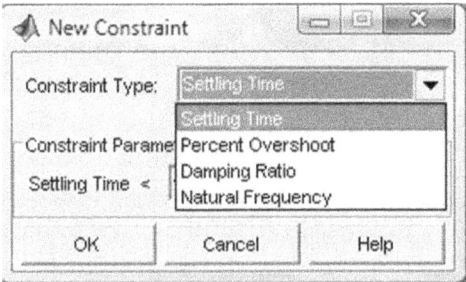

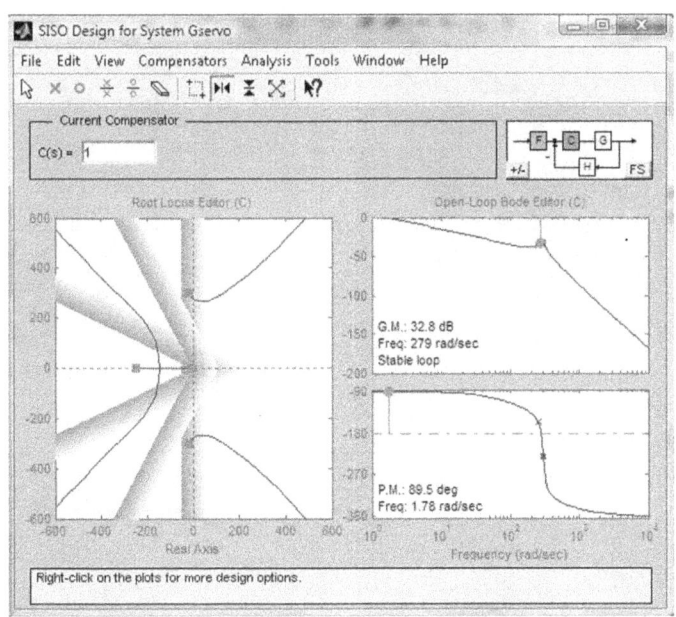

Notice: for each design constraints, press "ok "and then open the design constraint again to put the other constraint values.

Step#5: LTI viewer

Go analysis icon and select other loop response icon.

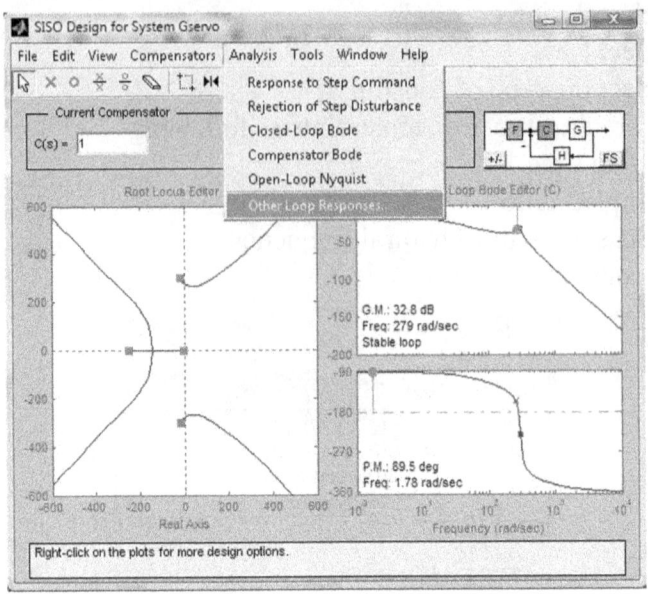

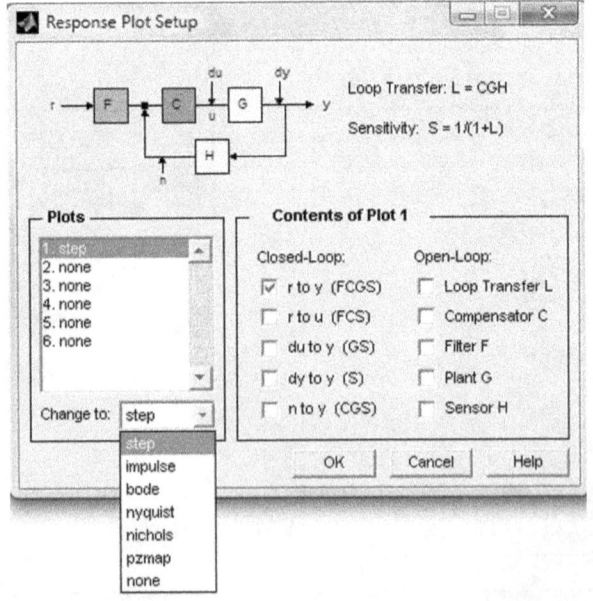

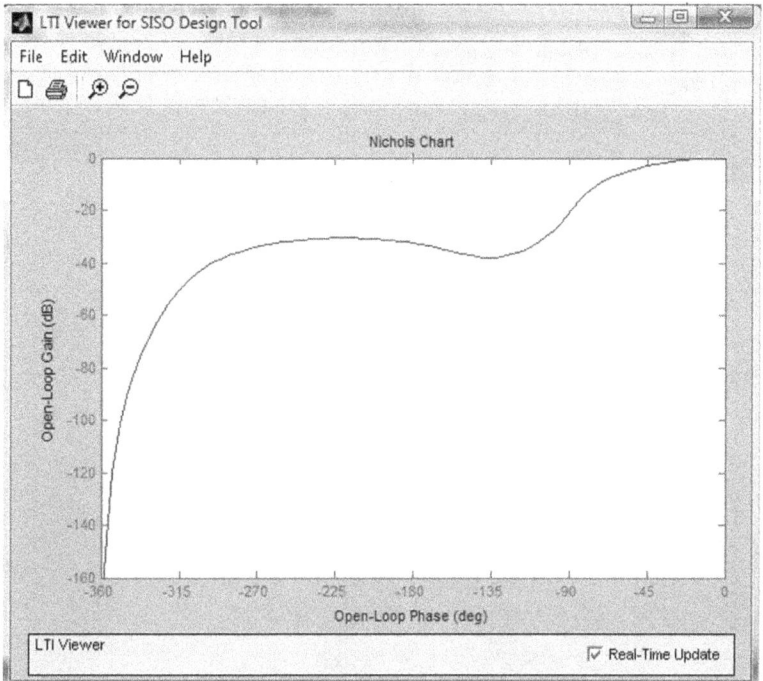

6.8. Adding Plots of Basic Statistics to Graphs

The MATLAB Statistics tool computes basic statistics such as max, min, average, mode,...etc. which are plotted in a graph and then plots these statistics in the same graph.

Example (53): find the basic statistics date, max, min, average, for this saved data for population (census) data. (This example just to show how MATLAB is able to calculate the average, standard deviation, and others statistics parameters from a group of reported or input data)

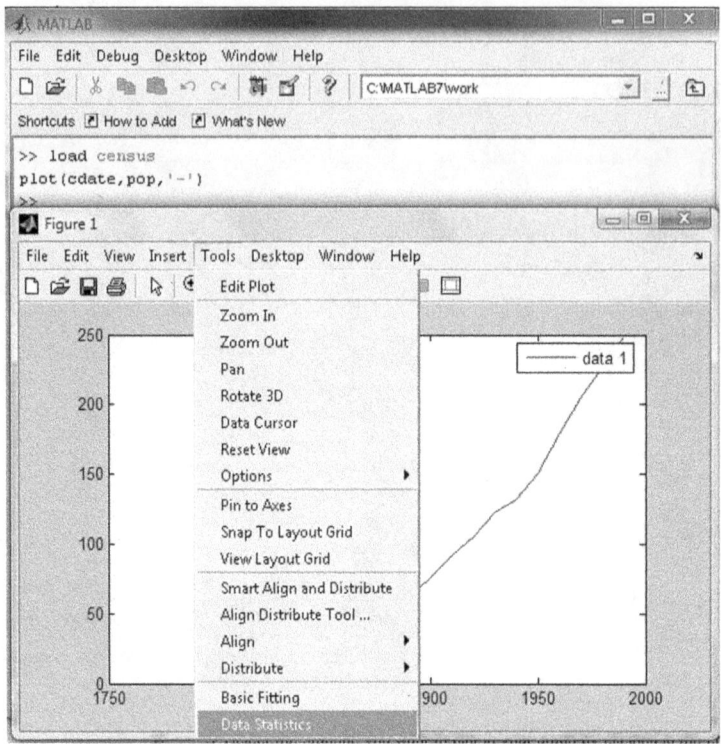

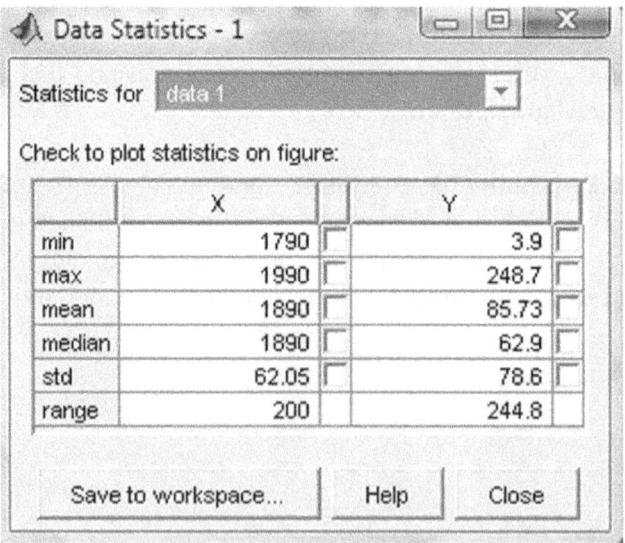

A "min" is the minimum value, a "max" is the maximum value, and "std" is the standard deviation. The rang is the difference between the maximum and the minimum value. The mean is the average.

If you choose one of those statistics data, it will be showed up on the figure. For example, we will choose std, mean and median.

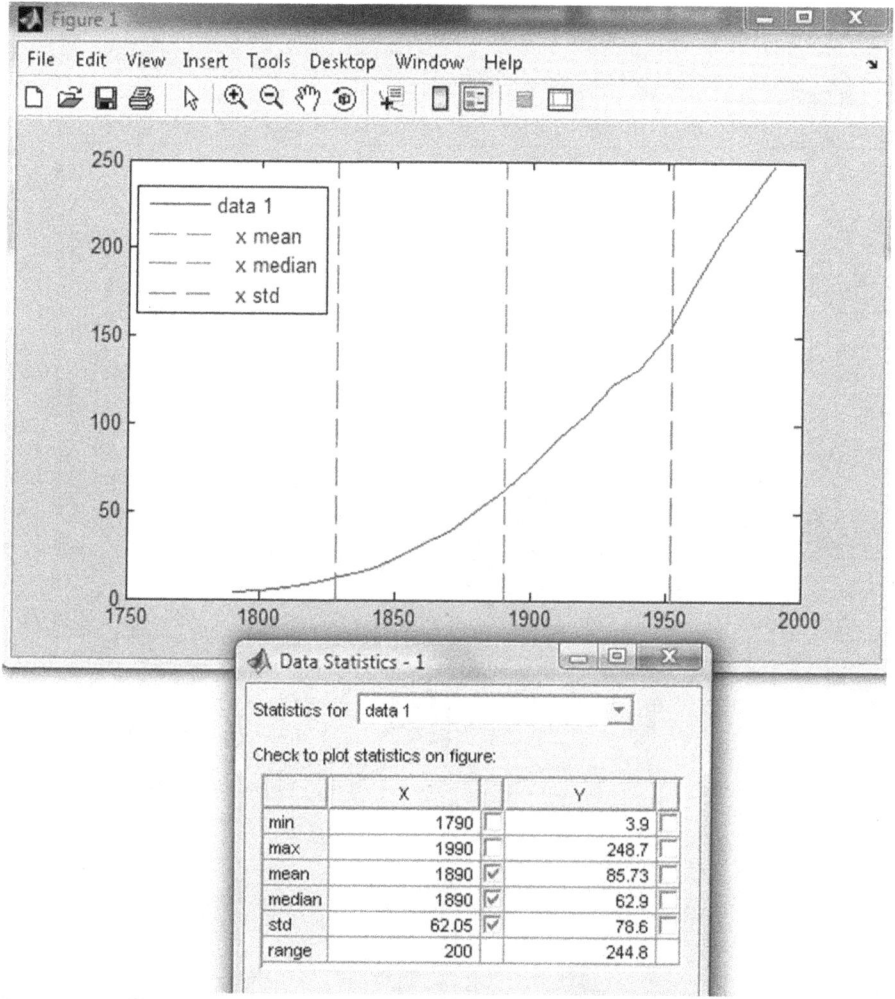

6.9. Simulation of Chemical Reaction by using (rsmdemo).

The" rsmdemo" is a MATLAB command which provides the design of experiments and surface fitting through the simulation of a chemical reaction by comparing results from trial-and-error data and designed/reported experimental data.

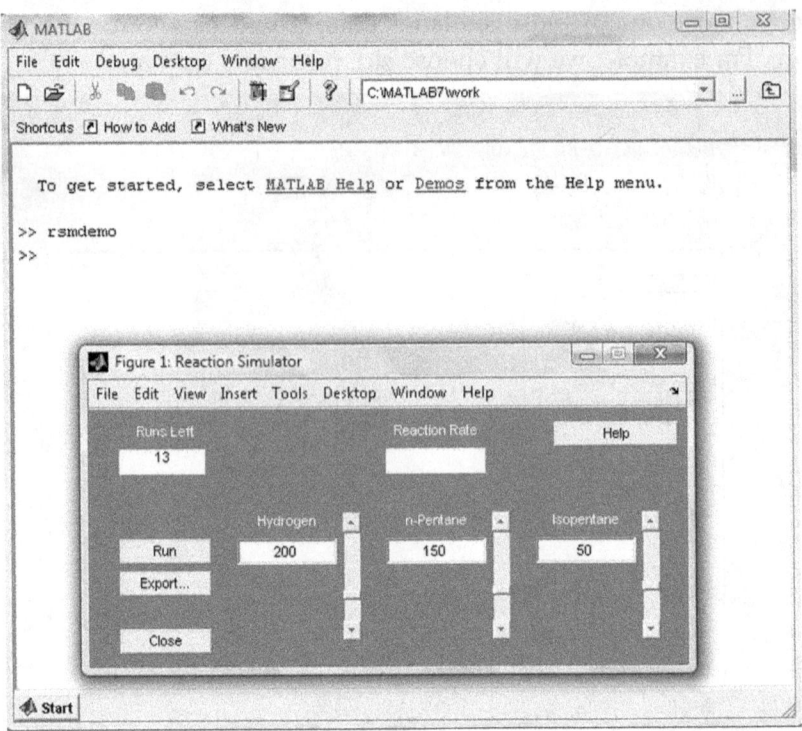

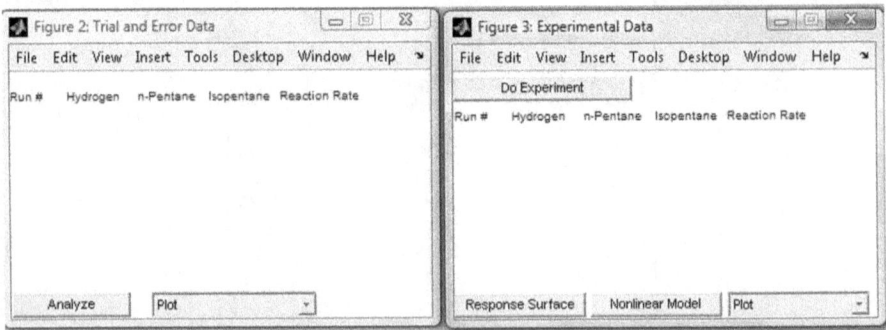

From experimental Data window, you can do your experiment.

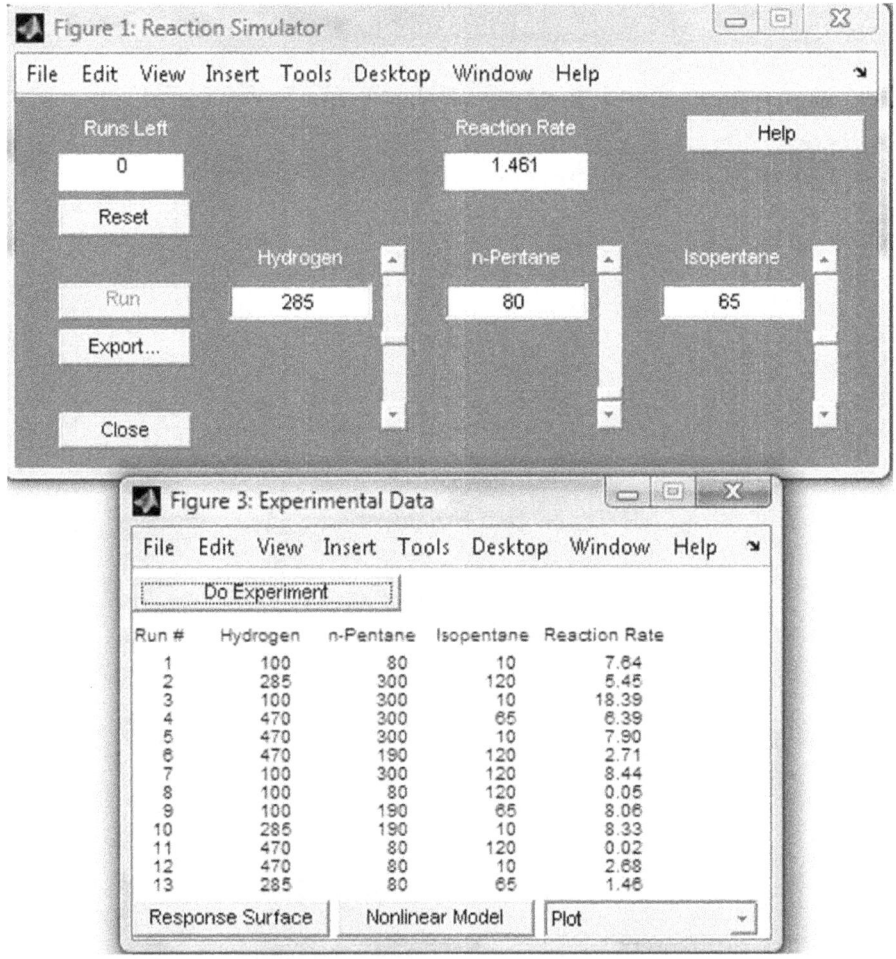

You can plot the data of the experiment for example hydrogen vs rate. Also, we can change the comparing method from the experimental data, too.

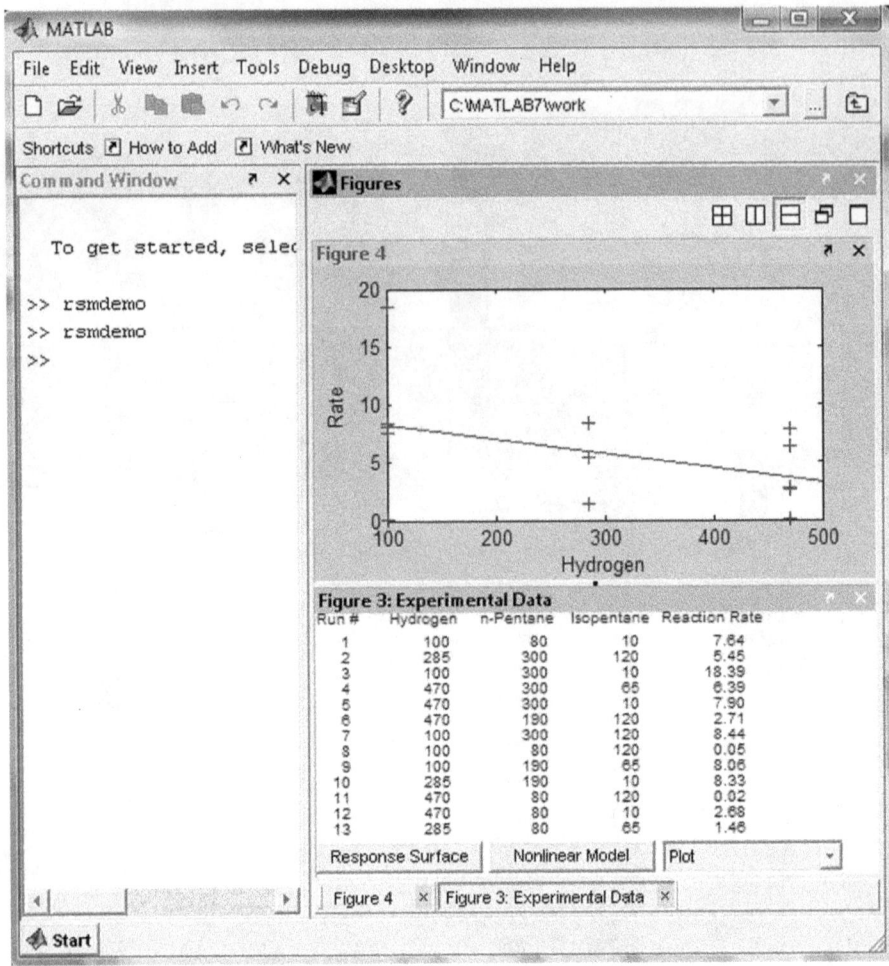

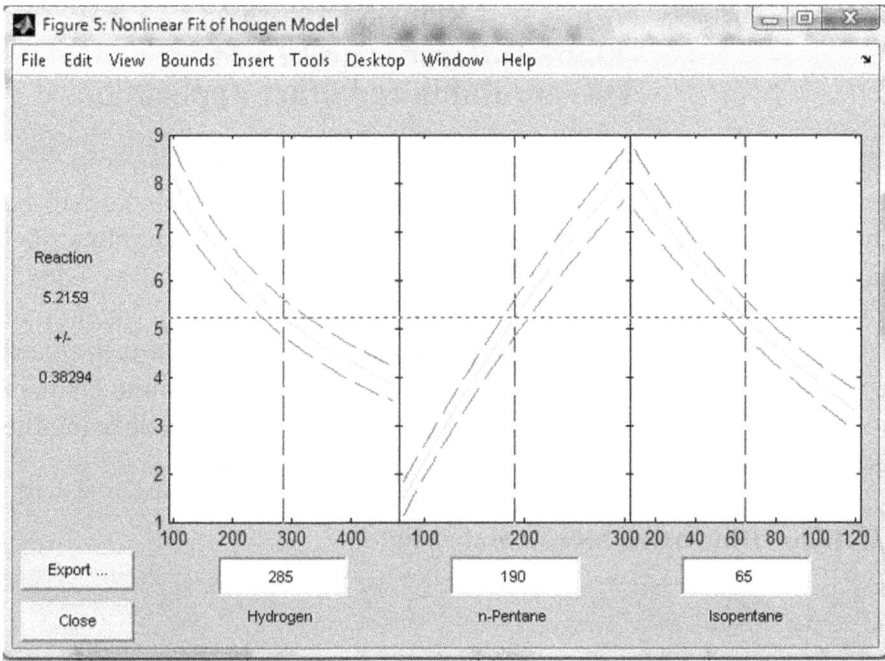

Response surface figure

Shortcuts [?] How to Add [?] What's New

```
>> pi

ans =

    3.1416

>> sqrt(27)

ans =

    5.1962

>> 24^(34-2)

ans =

  1.4681e+044

>> sin(pi/2)
```

CHAPTER #7: Numerical Solution Using MATLAB -Finite Difference and FEM for Thermo-fluids and other applications

The Diffusion Models

In this chapter, the one and two-dimensional diffusion model will be mentioned either in steady state or transient using different numerical methods. MATLAB has different "ode" command such as ode45. Those commands are available and applicable in any version of MATLAB This chapter will cover the solution numerical techniques using finite difference method (FDM) as well as using Finite element method (FEM). In some examples, we will validate our code using the analytical solution.

7.1.1. One Dimension Steady State Model

$$k\frac{\partial^2 \phi}{\partial x^2} = \rho c \frac{\partial \phi}{\partial t}$$

$$(7.1)$$

Here, φ is known as the dependent variable which might represent temperature, velocity, or species.

The equation (7.1) can be solved analytically as

$$\phi = ax + b$$

$$(7.2)$$

Where a and b are constants, and they can be evaluated from the boundary conditions.

Example (54): Find the temperature distribution of the 1D steady state bounded slab numerically and analytically at x=0, T=100°C and at x=L, T=40°C.

$$\frac{\partial^2 T}{\partial x^2} = 0$$

$$T = ax + b$$

Using normalization as

$$\theta = \frac{T - T_h}{T_h - T_c}, \quad X = \frac{x}{L}, \frac{\partial^2 \theta}{\partial X^2} = 0$$

The pervious temperature distribution becomes:

$\theta(0) = 1, \theta(1) = 0$ After applying the boundary conditions, the equation becomes

$$\theta = -X + 1 \tag{7.3}$$

The numerical solution of this type of problem
Using central finite difference

$$\frac{\partial^2 \theta}{\partial X^2} = 0$$

$$\frac{\theta(i+1) - 2\theta(i) + \theta(i-1)}{\Delta X^2} = 0$$

$$\theta(i) = \frac{\theta(i+1) + \theta(i-1)}{2}$$

Using MATLAB to solve the analytical and numerical problem as

```
% 1D heat diffusion
% 1.Setting up the boundary condition
% 2.Calculating of the analytical solution
% 3.Using Central Finite Difference
% 4.Iterative numerical Tech. has been used
clear all
clc
Nx=50; % Number of nodes in x-direction
X=0:1/(Nx-1):1;
% Initialization and Number of iterations
Theat=zeros(Nx);
mstep=1000;
% 1. Boundary Conditions
Theta(1)=1; % Normalized temperature
Theta(Nx)=0;
```

```
% 2. Analytical Solution
for i=1:Nx
        Thetaa(i)=-X(i)+1;
end
for kk=1:mstep

        for i=2:Nx-1
            Theta(i)=0.5*(Theta(i-1)+Theta(i+1));
        end
end
plot(X,Thetaa,'r')
hold on
plot(X,Theta,'*')
hold off
legend('Analytical solution','Numerical solution')
title('Temperature Profile of One Dimension Bounded Slab')
xlabel('Number of nodes');
ylabel('Normalized Temperature(Dimensionless)')
```

The above code is used to solve one dimension steady state heat diffusion problem.
It can be modified to be used for transient one dimension heat diffusion problem.

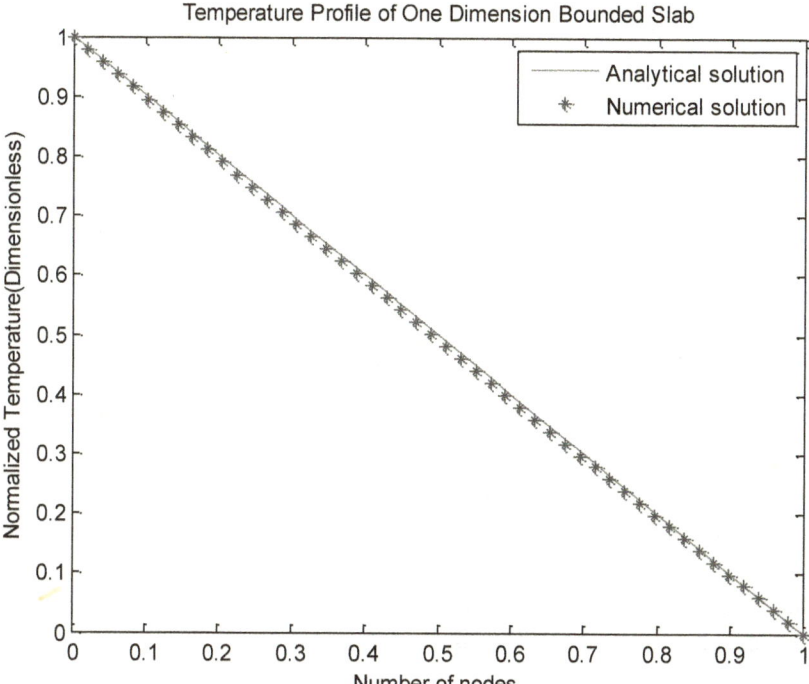

Figure(7.1). illustrates the numerical and the analytical solution of 1D diffusion steady state

One dimension steady state model with heat generation

$$k\frac{\partial^2 T}{\partial x^2} = -\dot{q}$$

$$(7.4)$$

After doing normalization the equation (7.4) becomes

$$\frac{\partial^2 \theta}{\partial X^2} = -\frac{\dot{q}\,L^2}{k(Th - Tc)}$$

The left hand side terms represents the normalized heat generation Q

$$\frac{\partial^2 \theta}{\partial X^2} = -Q$$

If we assume Q=0.5 (dimensionless values), the numerical solution becomes as following

Solving the pervious equation (7.4) using numerical and analytical can be done here

Numerical Solution

$$\frac{\theta(i+1) - 2\theta(i) + \theta(i-1)}{\Delta X^2} = -Q$$

$$\theta(i) = \frac{1}{2} Q \Delta X^2 + \frac{1}{2}(\theta(i-1) - \theta(i-1))$$

Using MATLAB to solve the problem numerically

```
% 1D heat diffusion" Heat generation"
% 1.Setting up the boundary condition
% 2.Calculating of the analytical solution
% 3.Using Central Finite Difference
% 4.Iterative numerical Tech. has been used
clear all
clc
Nx=100; % Number of nodes in x-direction
X=0:1/(Nx-1):1;
% Initialization and Number of iterations
Theta=zeros(Nx);
mstep=1000;
dx=1/(Nx-1)
% 1. Boundary Conditions
Theta(1)=1; % Normalized temperature
Theta(Nx)=0;
Q=0.5; % Normalized heat generation
for kk=1:mstep

        for i=2:Nx-1
            Theta(i)=0.5*Q*dx+0.5*(Theta(i-1)+Theta(i+1));
        end
end

plot(X,Theta,'*')
```

legend('Numerical solution')
title('Temperature Profile of One Dimension Bounded Slab with heat Generation')
xlabel('Number of nodes');
ylabel('Normalized Temperature(Dimensionless)')

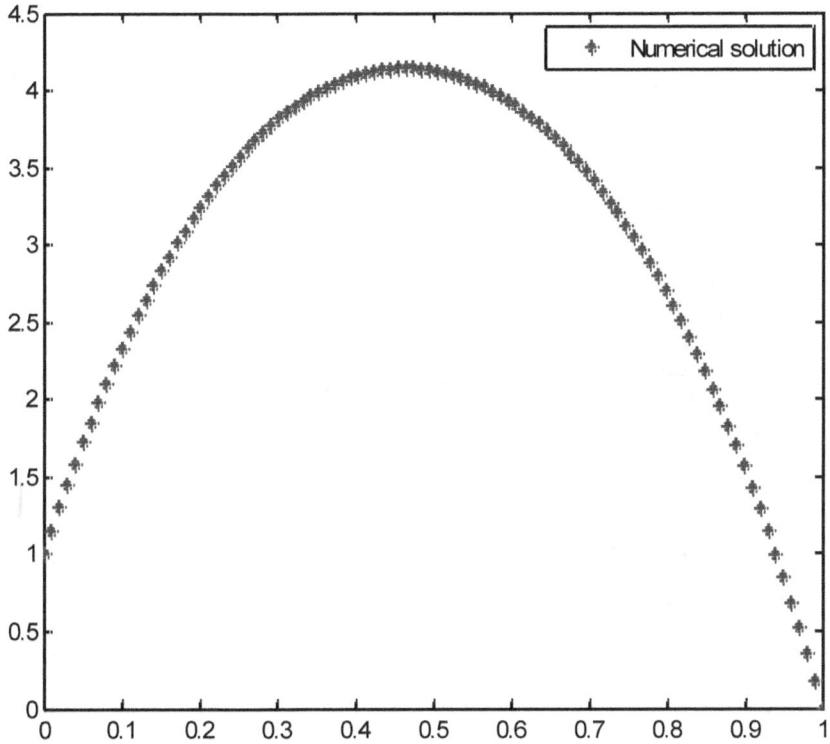

Figure(7.2). illustrates the numerical solution of 1D diffusion steady state model with heat generation

7.1.2. One Dimensional Transient Diffusion Model

One dimensional diffusion transient equation can be written as

$$k \frac{\partial^2 \phi}{\partial x^2} = \rho c \frac{\partial \phi}{\partial t}$$

(7.5)

Here, φ is known as the dependent variable which might represent temperature, velocity, or species. The diffusion process becomes faster as the κ increases and vice versa where, κ is either thermal diffusivity or kinematic viscosity. For scaling purpose τ is the time scale and L is the scale of length; therefore

$$\frac{\partial^2 \varphi}{\partial x^2} = \frac{\rho c}{k} \frac{\partial \varphi}{\partial t}$$

From equation 7.5 the length scale is proportional to $L = \sqrt{\alpha \tau}$
Equation 5.1 has second derivative in space; so that, the equation needs two boundaries conditions to be solved and also it needs the initial condition.

Example (55) one –dimensional momentum diffusion for a fluid confined betweentwoparallelplatesareduetothemotionoftheupperlidcanbewrittenas

$$\upsilon \frac{\partial^2 u}{\partial x^2} = \frac{\partial u}{\partial t}$$

$$(7.6)$$

From the equation 7.6, the rate of momentum diffusion relies on the viscosity of the fluid and the distance between two parallel plates.

$$\frac{F}{A} = \mu \frac{\partial u}{\partial y}$$

The finite Difference approximation can be applied (forward for time and central differences in space) here easily:

$$\frac{u^{t+1}(i) - u^t(i)}{\Delta t} = \upsilon \frac{u(i+1) - 2u(i) + u(i-1)}{\Delta x^2}$$

$$u^{t+1}(i) = \frac{\Delta t}{\Delta x^2} \upsilon (u^t(i+1) - 2u^t(i) + u^t(i-1)) + u^t(i)$$

$$(7.7)$$

For the stability condition (using explicit scheme), the coefficients in the right hand side must be greater than zero. Therefore, to satisfy this condition we should select

$$\Delta \tau = \frac{\Delta t}{\alpha L^2}$$

Where, $\upsilon = \frac{\mu}{\rho}$, For scaling:

The equation 7.7 becomes:

$$U^{\tau+1}(i) = U^{\tau}(1-\tau) + \tau \frac{U^{\tau}(i+1) + U^{\tau}(i-1)}{2}$$

Example (56). Find the temperature distribution of 1D diffusion transient heat transfer. The boundary conditions are at x=0 T=100C, and x=L is T=40C and initial temperature is zero.

$$\frac{\theta^{t+1}(i) - \theta^{t}(i)}{\Delta \tau} = \frac{\theta^{t}(i+1) - 2\theta^{t}(i) + \theta^{t}(i-1)}{\Delta X^2}$$

$$\Delta \tau = \frac{\Delta t}{\alpha L^2}, \quad \alpha = \frac{k}{\rho c}$$

$$\theta^{t+1}(i) = \frac{\Delta \tau}{\Delta X^2}[\theta^{t}(i+1) - 2\theta^{t}(i) + \theta^{t}(i-1)] + \theta^{t}(i)$$

```
% 1. one dimensional tansient
% 2. Number of nodes in x direction
% 3. Initialization
% 4. setting up the initial and BCs
% 5. Total number of iteration
Nx=100;
Theta=zeros(Nx); % Temperature distribution at future time
Thetao=zeros(Nx); % Temperature distribution at current time
% Setting the BCs
Thetao(1)=1;
Thetao(Nx)=0;
Theta(1)=1;
Theta(Nx)=0;
% Total number of iterations
Tau=0.00001;
DX=1/(Nx-1);
mstep=1000;
X=0:1/(Nx-1):1;
```

```
for kk=1:mstep
        for i=2:Nx-1
              Theta(i)=Tau/DX.^2*(Thetao(i+1)-2*Thetao(i)+Thetao(i-
              1))+Thetao(i);
        end

% For update
Thetao=Theta;
end
plot(X,Theta);
legend('1D Transient Heat Diffusion')
xlabel('Number of Grids');ylabel('Normalized Temperature Profile')
```

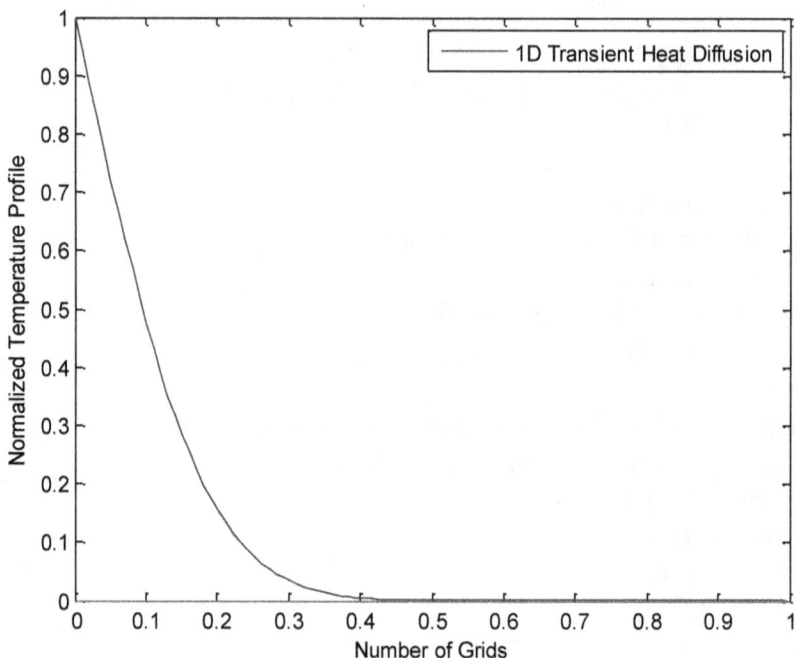

Figure(7.3). illustrates the numerical solution of 1D diffusion transient model

Here, the heat generation can be added as we have done in the steady state 1D diffusion problem.

The governor equation will be :

$$\theta^{l+1}(i) = \frac{\Delta\tau}{\Delta X^2}[\theta^l(i+1) - 2\theta^l(i) + \theta^l(i-1)] + \theta^l(i) + \Delta\tau Q$$

Where Q is the normalized heat generation as it is defined in the previous example.

If the heat generation is increased, it will affect one the temperature distribution over the 1D slab.

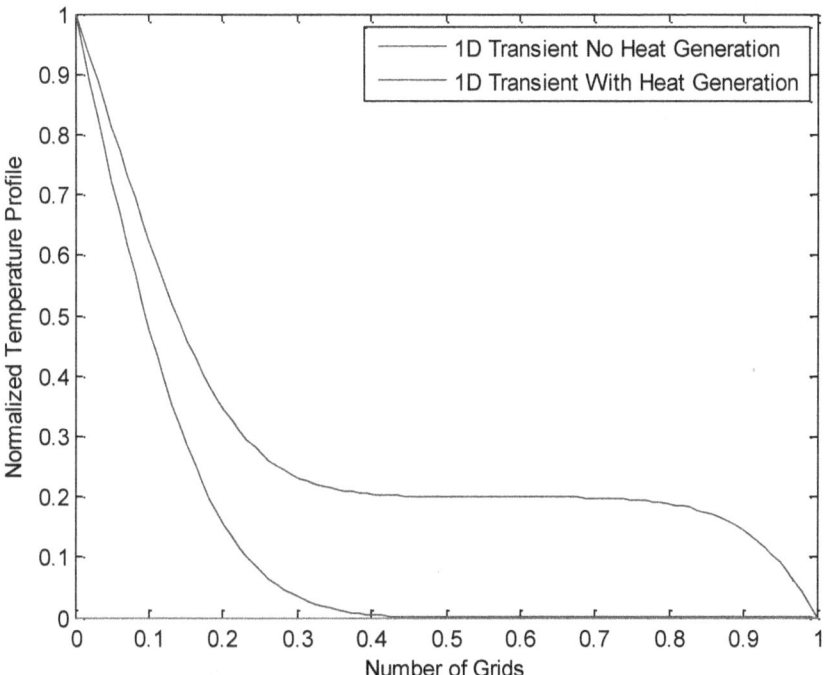

Figure(7.4). Illustrates the numerical solution of 1D diffusion transient model with and w/o heat generation.

% 1. one dimensional transient
% 2. Number of nodes in x direction
% 3. Initialization
% 4. setting up the initial and BCs
% 5. Total number of iteration
Nx=100;
Theta=zeros(Nx); % Temperature distribution at future time
Thetao=zeros(Nx); % Temperature distribution at current time
% Setting the BCs
Thetao(1)=1;
Thetao(Nx)=0;
Theta(1)=1;
Theta(Nx)=0;

```
% Setting BCs for
Theta1=zeros(Nx); % Temperature distribution at future time
Thetao1=zeros(Nx); % Temperature distribution at current time
% Setting the BCs
Thetao1(1)=1;
Thetao1(Nx)=0;
Theta1(1)=1;
Theta1(Nx)=0;
% Total number of iterations
Tau=0.00001;
DX=1/(Nx-1);
mstep=1000;
X=0:1/(Nx-1):1;
Q=20;
for kk=1:mstep
        for i=2:Nx-1
                Theta(i)=Tau/DX.^2*(Thetao(i+1)-2*Thetao(i)+Thetao(i-
                1))+Thetao(i);
        end
        for i=2:Nx-1
                Theta1(i)=Tau/DX.^2*(Thetao1(i+1)-
                2*Thetao1(i)+Thetao1(i-1))+Thetao1(i)+Tau*Q;
        end

        % For update temperature
        Thetao=Theta;
        Thetao1=Theta1;
end
plot(X,Theta,'b');
hold on
plot(X,Theta1,'--');
legend('1D Transient No Heat Generation','1D Transient With Heat Generation')
hold off
xlabel('Number of Grids');ylabel('Normalized Temperature Profile')
```

In case of increasing the heat generation 3 times, the temperature distribution will jump up:

The governing equation will be:

$$\theta^{l+1}(i) = \frac{\Delta\tau}{\Delta X^2}[\theta^l(i+1) - 2\theta^l(i) + \theta^l(i-1)] + \theta^l(i) + \Delta\tau Q$$

Selecting the time step and number of grids are important to be sure the code is stable.

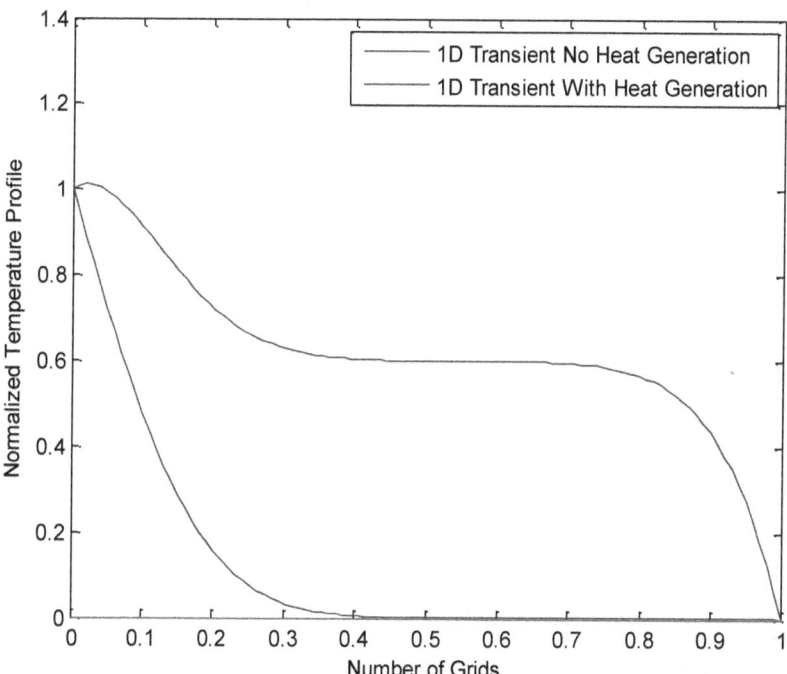

--- *With heat generation*
___ *No heat generation*

Figure(7.5). The temperature distribution of 1D transient with and w/o heat generation (Q=60)

7.2.1. Two dimensional steady state diffusion

For isotropic material when $k_x = k_y$ (in two dimensions). The steady state heat transfer can be governed by

$$\frac{\partial^2 T}{\partial x^2} + \frac{\partial^2 T}{\partial y^2} = 0$$

(7.8)

In case of a material is non-isotropic when $k_x \neq k_y$. The steady state heat transfer can be governed by :

$$\frac{\partial^2 T}{\partial x^2} + \frac{k_y}{k_x}\frac{\partial^2 T}{\partial y^2} = 0$$

(7.9)

After normalizing the two-dimensional equation (7.9) yields

$$\frac{\partial^2 T}{\partial x^2} + \frac{k_y}{k_x}\frac{\partial^2 T}{\partial y^2} = 0$$

The material is uniform in every orientation (isotropic)

$$\frac{\partial^2 \theta}{\partial X^2} + \frac{k_y}{k_x}\left(\frac{L}{H}\right)^2 \frac{\partial^2 \theta}{\partial Y^2} = 0$$

(7.10)

Discretizing the equation (7.10) using central finite difference yields

$$2\left(\frac{1}{\Delta X^2} + \frac{1}{\Delta Y^2}\right)\theta(i,j) = \frac{1}{\Delta X^2}(\theta(j,i+1) + \theta(j,i-1)) + \frac{AR^2}{\Delta Y^2}(\theta(j+1,i) + \theta(j-1,i))$$

$$\theta(i,j) = \frac{1}{2\left(\frac{1}{\Delta X^2} + \frac{1}{\Delta Y^2}\right)}\{\frac{1}{\Delta X^2}(\theta(j,i+1) + \theta(j,i-1)) + \frac{AR^2}{\Delta Y^2}(\theta(j+1,i) + \theta(j-1,i))\}$$

Example (57): Find the temperature profile for the following square block in case
   a. Isotropic material
   b. Non-isotropic material

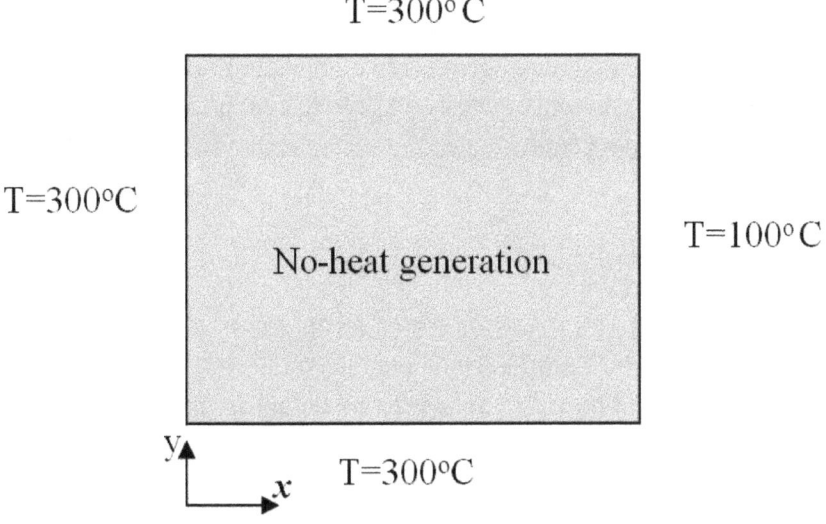

$$\theta = \frac{T - Tc}{T_h - T_c}, \ X = \frac{x}{L}, Y = \frac{y}{H}$$

Using central finite difference

$$\theta(i,j) = \frac{1}{2(\frac{1}{\Delta X^2} + \frac{AR^2}{\Delta Y^2})} \{\frac{1}{\Delta X^2}(\theta(j,i+1) + \theta(j,i-1)) + \frac{AR^2}{\Delta Y^2}(\theta(j+1,i) + \theta(j-1,i))\}$$

%1. 2D Diffusion model
%2. Setting numbre of grids in x and y-direction
%3. Setting the BCs
%4. Initialization of the Domain
%5. Iterative loop
Nx=100;
Ny=100;
%:.........................
X=0:1/(Nx-1):1;
Y=0:1/(Ny-1):1;
Theta=zeros(Nx,Ny);
% Setting up the BCs
Theta(:,1)=1; % Left BCs
Theta(:,Nx)=0; % Right BCs
Theta(1,:)=1; % Lower BCs
Theta(Ny,:)=1; % Upper BCs

```matlab
%::::::::::::::::::::::::::::::::::
mstep=1000; % Total Number of iterations
dX=1/(Nx-1);% The distance between two adjacent node in x-direction
dY=1/(Ny-1);% The distance between two adjacent nodes in y-direction
AR=Nx/Ny; % Aspect ratio
for kk=1:mstep

        for i=2:Nx-1
          for j=2:Ny-1
            Theta(j,i)=1/(2*(1/dX.^2+1/dY.^2))*(1/
            dX.^2*(Theta(j,i+1)+Theta(j,i-1))...
            +AR.^2/dY.^2*(Theta(j+1,i)+Theta(j-1,i)));
          end
        end
end
figure(1)
contourf(Theta);
xlabel('Number of grids in x-direction');
ylabel('number of grid in y-direction');
figure(2)
plot(Y,Theta(:,50),'ko')
hold on
plot(Y,Theta(:,60),'--')
plot(Y,Theta(:,80))
hold off
xlabel('Y');ylabel('Normalized Temperature')
legend('X=0.5','X=0.6','X=0.8')
```

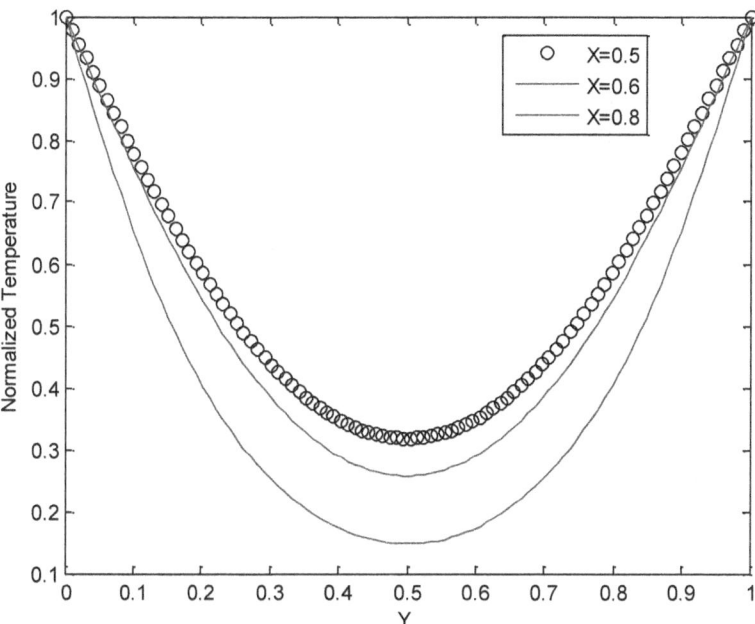

Figure(7.6). The temperature distribution at various cross-section of 2D steady state for isotropic material

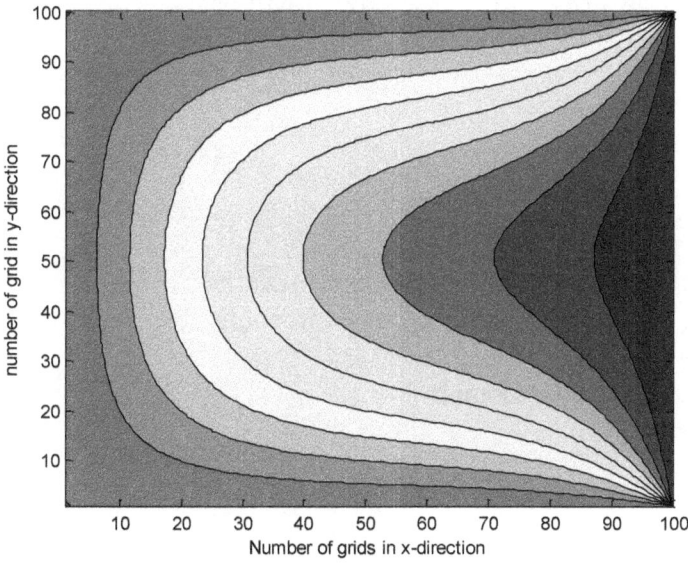

Figure(7.7). The temperature distribution contour of 2D steady state for isotropic material

For non-isotropic material

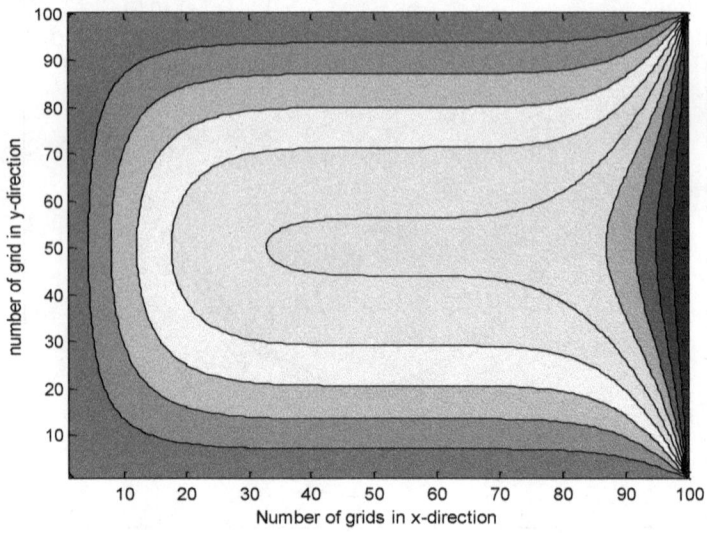

Figure(7.8). The temperature distribution contour of 2D steady state for non-isotropic material

Non-isotropic governing after discretizing will be

$$\theta(i,j) = \frac{1}{2(\frac{1}{\Delta X^2} + \frac{AR^2}{\Delta Y^2} \times K)} \{\frac{1}{\Delta X^2}(\theta(j,i+1) + \theta(j,i-1)) + \frac{AR^2}{\Delta Y^2} \times K(\theta(j+1,i) + \theta(j-1,i))\}$$

Where $K = \dfrac{k_y}{k_x}$

```
%1. 2D Diffusion model for non-isotropic material
%2. Setting number of grids in x and y-direction
%3. Setting the BCs
%4. Initialization of the Domain
%5. Iterative loop
Nx=100;
Ny=100;
%:........................
X=0:1/(Nx-1):1;
Y=0:1/(Ny-1):1;
Theta=zeros(Nx,Ny);
% Setting up the BCs
```

```matlab
Theta(:,1)=1; % Left BCs
Theta(:,Nx)=0; % Right BCs
Theta(1,:)=1; % Lower BCs
Theta(Ny,:)=1; % Upper BCs
%::::::::::::::::::::::::::::::
mstep=1000; % Total Number of iterations
dX=1/(Nx-1);% The distance between two adjacent node in x-direction
dY=1/(Ny-1);% The distance between two adjacent nodes in y-direction
AR=Nx/Ny; % Aspect ratio
K=10; % Thermal conductivity ratio (dimensionless)
for kk=1:mstep

        for i=2:Nx-1
          for j=2:Ny-1
             Theta(j,i)=1/(2*(1/dX.^2+(AR.^2*K)/dY.^2))*(1/
             dX.^2*(Theta(j,i+1)+Theta(j,i-1))...
             +(AR.^2*K)/dY.^2*(Theta(j+1,i)+Theta(j-1,i)));
          end
        end
end
figure(1)
contourf(Theta);
xlabel('Number of grids in x-direction');
ylabel('number of grid in y-direction');
figure(2)
plot(Y,Theta(:,50),'ko')
hold on
plot(Y,Theta(:,60),'--')
plot(Y,Theta(:,80))
hold off
xlabel('Y');ylabel('Normalized Temperature')
legend('X=0.5','X=0.6','X=0.8')
```

Example (58): Find the temperature profile for the following square block in case
   a. Isotropic material
   b. Non-isotropic material

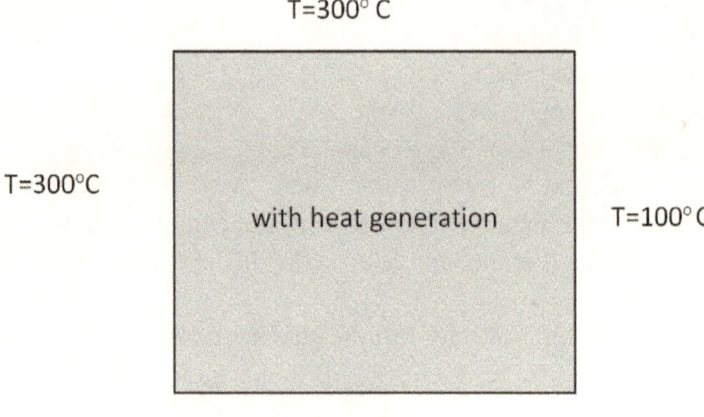

Isotropic governing after discretizing will be

$$\theta(i,j) = \frac{1}{2(\frac{1}{\Delta X^2} + \frac{AR^2}{\Delta Y^2})} \{ \frac{1}{\Delta X^2}(\theta(j,i+1) + \theta(j,i-1)) + \frac{AR^2}{\Delta Y^2}(\theta(j+1,i) + \theta(j-1,i)) + Q \}$$

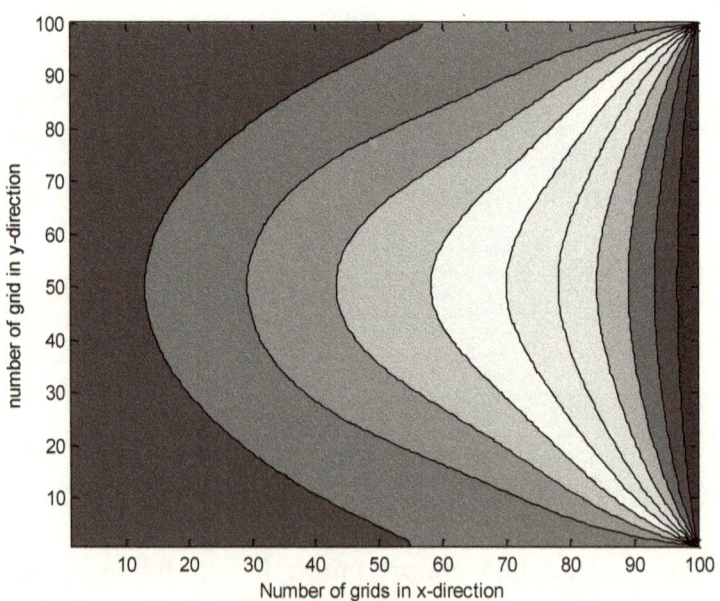

Figure(7.9). The temperature distribution contour of 2D steady state for isotropic material with heat generation

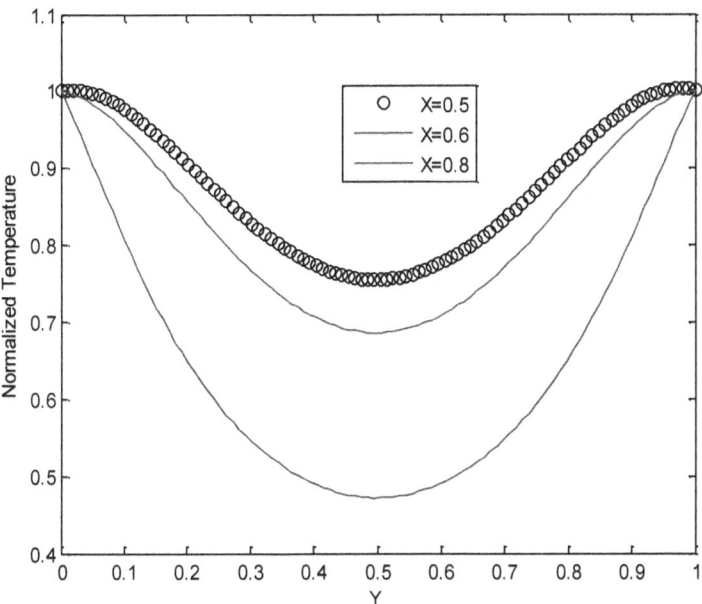

Figure(7.10). The temperature distribution at various cross-sections of 2D steady state for isotropic material with heat generation.

b.

```
%1. 2D Diffusion model
%2. Setting numbre of grids in x and y-direction
%3. Setting the BCs
%4. Initialization of the Domain
%5. Iterative loop
Nx=100;
Ny=100;
%:..........................
X=0:1/(Nx-1):1;
Y=0:1/(Ny-1):1;
Theta=zeros(Nx,Ny);
% Setting up the BCs
Theta(:,1)=1; % Left BCs
Theta(:,Nx)=0; % Right BCs
Theta(1,:)=1; % Lower BCs
Theta(Ny,:)=1; % Upper BCs
%:............................
mstep=1000; % Total Number of iterations
dX=1/(Nx-1);% The distance between two adjacent node in x-direction
dY=1/(Ny-1);% The distance between two adjacent nodes in y-direction
AR=Nx/Ny; % Aspect ratio
K=3; % Thermal conductivity ratio (dimensionless)
Q=10; % Heat Generation Dimensionless
for kk=1:mstep

        for i=2:Nx-1
          for j=2:Ny-1
             Theta(j,i)=1/(2*(1/dX.^2+(AR.^2*K)/dY.^2))*(1/
             dX.^2*(Theta(j,i+1)+Theta(j,i-1))...
             +(AR.^2*K)/dY.^2*(Theta(j+1,i)+Theta(j-1,i))+Q);
          end
        end
end
figure(1)
contourf(Theta);
xlabel('Number of grids in x-direction');
ylabel('number of grid in y-direction');
```

```
figure(2)
plot(Y,Theta(:,50),'ko')
hold on
plot(Y,Theta(:,60),'--')
plot(Y,Theta(:,80))
hold off
xlabel('Y');ylabel('Normalized Temperature')
legend('X=0.5','X=0.6','X=0.8')
```

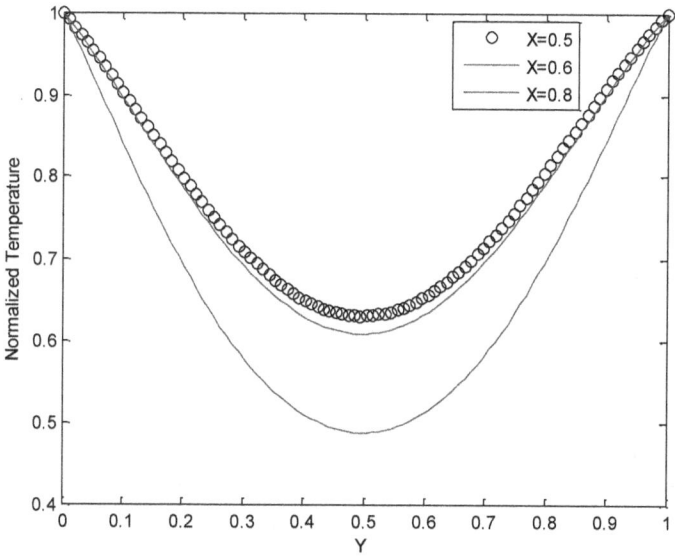

Figure(7.11). The temperature distribution at various cross-sections of 2D steady state for non-isotropic material with heat generation.

7.2.2. Two dimensional transient heat transfer diffusion

The two dimensional transient diffusion heat transfer is governed by

$$k_x \frac{\partial^2 T}{\partial x^2} + k_y \frac{\partial^2 T}{\partial y^2} = \rho c \frac{\partial T}{\partial t}$$

(7.10)

For isotropic material $k_y = k_y$

$$\frac{\partial^2 T}{\partial x^2} + \frac{\partial^2 T}{\partial y^2} = \frac{1}{\alpha} \frac{\partial T}{\partial t}$$

For non-isotropic material $k_y \neq k_y$

$$\frac{\partial^2 T}{\partial x^2} + \frac{k_y}{k_x}\frac{\partial^2 T}{\partial y^2} = \frac{1}{\alpha_x}\frac{\partial T}{\partial t} \tag{7.11}$$

$$\kappa = \frac{k_y}{k_x} \text{ is thermal conductivity ratio (dimensionless)}$$

$$\frac{\partial^2 T}{\partial x^2} + \kappa\frac{\partial^2 T}{\partial y^2} = \frac{1}{\alpha_x}\frac{\partial T}{\partial t}$$

If the material is isotropic, the thermal conductivity ratio is 1 and the pervious equation becomes after scaling is

$$\frac{\partial^2 \theta}{\partial X^2} + AR^2\frac{\partial^2 \theta}{\partial Y^2} = \frac{1}{\alpha}\frac{\partial \theta}{\partial t}$$

Using explicit method as

$$\frac{\theta^\tau(j,i+1) - 2\theta^\tau(j,i) + \theta^\tau(j,i-1)}{\Delta X^2} + AR^2\frac{\theta^\tau(j,i+1) - 2\theta^\tau(j,i) + \theta^\tau(j,i-1)}{\Delta Y^2} = \frac{\theta^{\tau+1}(j,i) - \theta^\tau(j,i)}{\Delta \tau}$$

$$\theta^{\tau+1}(j,i) = \Delta\tau \times [\frac{\theta^\tau(j,i+1) - 2\theta^\tau(j,i) + \theta^\tau(j,i-1)}{\Delta X^2} + AR^2\frac{\theta^\tau(j,i+1) - 2\theta^\tau(j,i) + \theta^\tau(j,i-1)}{\Delta Y^2}] + \theta^\tau(j,i)$$

Same as the example [7.5], but using transient explicit method with and w/o heat generation.

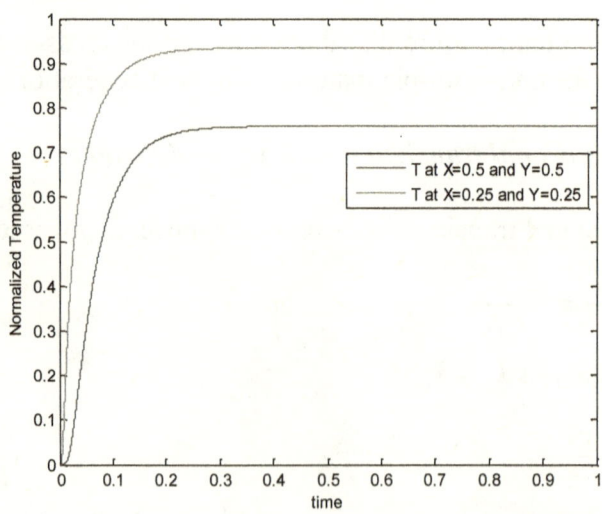

Figure(7.12). The temperature distribution at various cross-sections of 2D transient for isotropic material.

```matlab
%1. 2D Diffusion model
%2. Setting number of grids in x and y-direction
%3. Setting the BCs
%4. Initialization of the Domain
%5. Iterative loop
clear all
clc
Nx=50;
Ny=50;
%:.........................
X=0:1/(Nx-1):1;
Y=0:1/(Ny-1):1;
Thetao=zeros(Nx,Ny);
Theta=zeros(Nx,Ny);
% Setting up the BCs at current time
Thetao(:,1)=1; % Left BCs
Thetao(:,Nx)=0; % Right BCs
Thetao(1,:)=1; % Lower BCs
Thetao(Ny,:)=1; % Upper BCs
%Setting up the BCs at Future time
Theta(:,1)=1; % Left BCs
Theta(:,Nx)=0; % Right BCs
Theta(1,:)=1; % Lower BCs
Theta(Ny,:)=1; % Upper BCs
mstep=10000; % Total Number of iterations
dX=1/(Nx-1);% The distance between two adjacent node in x-direction
dY=1/(Ny-1);% The distance between two adjacent nodes in y-direction
AR=Nx/Ny; % Aspect ratio
K=3; % Thermal conductivity ratio (dimensionless)
Q=10; % Heat Generation Dimensionless
dt=0.0001;
for kk=1:mstep
        time(kk)=kk*dt;
        for i=2:Nx-1
            for j=2:Ny-1
```

```
        Theta(j,i)= dt*((Thetao(j,i+1)-2*Thetao(j,i)+Thetao(j,i-1))/
        dX.^2+...
        AR.^2*(Thetao(j+1,i)-2*Thetao(j,i)+Thetao(j-1,i))/
        dY.^2)+Thetao(j,i);
      end
    end
    Thetao=Theta;
    Temp1(kk)=Theta(Ny/2,Nx/2);
    Temp2(kk)=Theta(round(Ny/4),round(Nx/4));
end
figure(1)
contourf(Theta);
xlabel('Number of grids in x-direction');
ylabel('number of grid in y-direction');
figure(2)
plot(time,Temp1,'--')
hold on
plot(time,Temp2,'r')
hold off
legend ('T at X=0.5 and Y=0.5','T at X=0.25 and Y=0.25');
xlabel ('time');ylabel('Normalized Temperature');
```

With heat generation:

```
%1. 2D Diffusion model
%2. Setting numbre of grids in x and y-direction
%3. Setting the BCs
%4. Initialization of the Domain
%5. Iterative loop
clear all
clc
Nx=50;
Ny=50;
%:::::::::::::::::::::::::::
X=0:1/(Nx-1):1;
Y=0:1/(Ny-1):1;
Thetao=zeros(Nx,Ny);
Theta=zeros(Nx,Ny);
% Setting up the BCs at current time
Thetao(:,1)=1; % Left BCs
Thetao(:,Nx)=0; % Right BCs
Thetao(1,:)=1; % Lower BCs
Thetao(Ny,:)=1; % Upper BCs
%Setting up the BCs at Future time
Theta(:,1)=1; % Left BCs
Theta(:,Nx)=0; % Right BCs
Theta(1,:)=1; % Lower BCs
Theta(Ny,:)=1; % Upper BCs
mstep=10000; % Total Number of iterations
dX=1/(Nx-1);% The distance between two adjacent node in x-direction
dY=1/(Ny-1);% The distance between two adjacent nodes in y-direction
AR=Nx/Ny; % Aspect ratio
Q=10; % Heat Generation Dimensionless
dt=0.0001;
for kk=1:mstep
        time(kk)=kk*dt;
        for i=2:Nx-1
          for j=2:Ny-1
            Theta(j,i)= dt*((Thetao(j,i+1)-2*Thetao(j,i)+Thetao(j,i-1))/
            dX.^2+...
            AR.^2*(Thetao(j+1,i)-2*Thetao(j,i)+Thetao(j-1,i))/
            dY.^2)+Thetao(j,i)-dt*Q;
```

```
            end
        end
        Thetao=Theta;
        Temp1(kk)=Theta(Ny/2,Nx/2);
        Temp2(kk)=Theta(round(Ny/4),round(Nx/4));
end
figure(1)
contourf(Theta);
xlabel('Number of grids in x-direction');
ylabel('number of grid in y-direction');
figure(2)
plot(time,Temp1,'--')
hold on
plot(time,Temp2,'r')
hold off
legend ('T at X=0.5 and Y=0.5','T at X=0.25 and Y=0.25');
xlabel ('time');ylabel('Normalized Temperature');
```

In this code, we just added the heat generation in the main governing equation as

$$\theta^{\tau+1}(j,i) = \Delta\tau \times [\frac{\theta^{\tau}(j,i+1)-2\theta^{\tau}(j,i)+\theta^{\tau}(j,i-1)}{\Delta X^2} + AR^2 \frac{\theta^{\tau}(j,i+1)-2\theta^{\tau}(j,i)+\theta^{\tau}(j,i-1)}{\Delta Y^2}] + \theta^{\tau}(j,i) - \Delta\tau \times Q$$

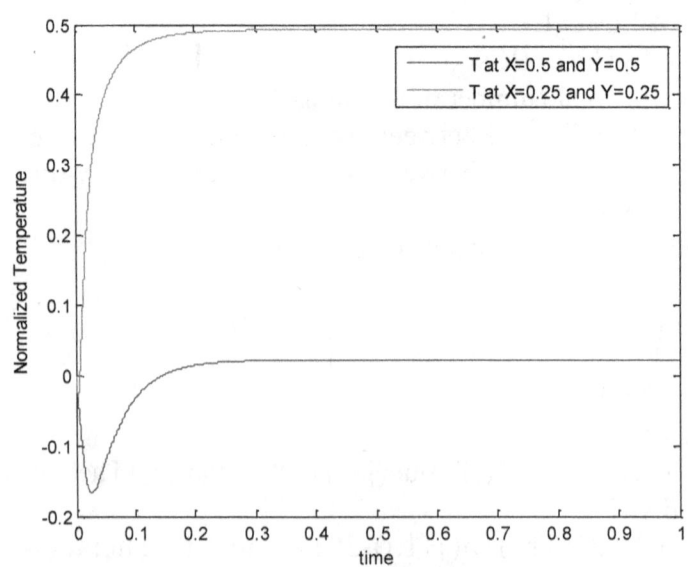

Figure(7.13). The temperature distribution at various cross-sections of 2D transient for isotropic material with heat generation.

Table7.1 Second order Approximations of the Finite difference schemes

Second order Finite Difference Scheme	
Forward scheme	$(\frac{\partial \theta}{\partial x})_i = \frac{\theta(i+1)-\theta(i)}{\Delta x}$
Backward scheme	$(\frac{\partial \theta}{\partial x})_i = \frac{\theta(i)-\theta(i-1)}{\Delta x}$
Central finite difference 1D (x-direction	$(\frac{\partial \theta}{\partial x})_i = \frac{\theta(i+1)-\theta(i-1)}{2\Delta x}$
Central finite difference 2D(x-direction)	$(\frac{\partial^2 \theta}{\partial x^2})_{i,j} = \frac{\theta(i+1,j)-2\theta(i,j)+\theta(i-1,j)}{(\Delta x)^2}$
Central finite difference 2D (y-direction)	$(\frac{\partial^2 \theta}{\partial y^2})_{i,j} = \frac{\theta(i,j+1)-2\theta(i,j)+\theta(i,j-1)}{(\Delta y)^2}$

7.2.3. Truss using FEM using MATLAB

The finite element is used to solve different engineering applications. This section will cover one dimensional bar with various cross-sectional areas when the external concentrated load exerted on the bar. Furthermore, the finite element is employed here to evaluate reaction force, stresses and elongation. The following two examples show how a programmer can use the MTALB to solve any engineering problems. FEM is a numerical technique and MATLAB is a tool to solve a problem.

Example (59): Determine the forces and stresses on each elements if E=30 x10⁶ Psi and A=2 in. The dispalcment at 2 is 0.05 in

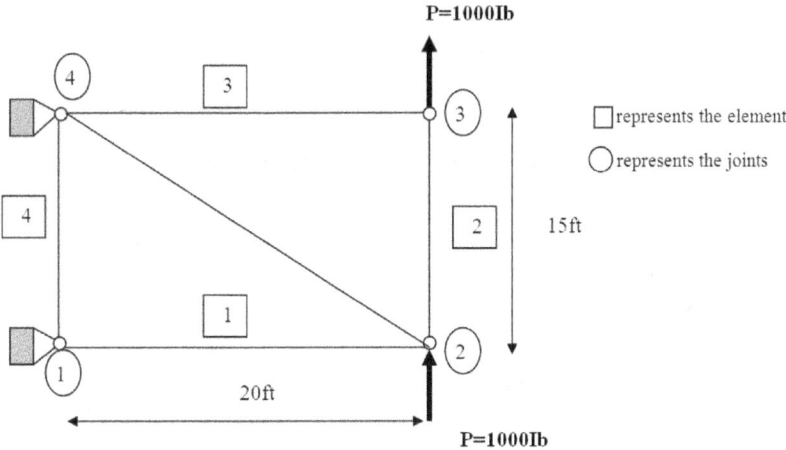

represents the element

represents the joints

```matlab
% Objective: This computer program computes the 2 truss
% clear memory
clear all
clc
% E; modulus of elasticity
% A: area of cross section
% L: length of bar
EA=1e7;
E=30e6;
% GENERATION OF COORDINATES AND CONDUCTIVITIES
nel=6; % number of elements
nonodes=4; % number of nodes
ielem=[1 2;1 3;4 2;3 2;4 3;4 1]; % IELEM Matrix
nodeCoor=[0 0;20*12 0;20*12 15*12;0 15*12];% Node Coordinates
xx=nodeCoor(:,1); % X POSITION FOR EACH NODE
yy=nodeCoor(:,2); % Y POSITION FOR EACH NODE
% FOR STRUCTURE
ndof=2*nonodes;
D=zeros(ndof,1); %DISPLACEMENT
force=zeros(ndof,1);% FORCE VECTOR
%EXTERNAL APPLIED FORCE
force(4)=1000;
force(6)=1000;
stiffness=zeros(ndof);
%BOUNDARY CONDITIONS LOCATION
prescribeddof=[1 2 7 8]';

% finding the global stiffness matrix
for i=1:nel
        indice=ielem(i,:);
        elementDof=[indice(1)*2-1 indice(1)*2 indice(2)*2-1 indice(2)*2];
        xa=xx(indice(2))-xx(indice(1));
        ya=yy(indice(2))-yy(indice(1));
        length_element=sqrt(xa^2+ya^2);
        C=xa/length_element;
        S=ya/length_element;
        k1=EA/length_element*[C*C C*S -C*C -C*S; C*S S*S -C*S -S*S;
           -C*C -C*S C*C C*S;-C*S -S*S C*S S*S];
```

```
        stiffness(elementDof,elementDof)=
            stiffness(elementDof,elementDof)+k1;
end
for i=1:2
        stiffnessl(1,i)=stiffness(1,i);
        stiffnessl(2,i)=stiffness(2,i);
end
        activeDof=setdiff([1:ndof]',[prescribeddof]);
        U=stiffness(activeDof,activeDof)\force(activeDof);
        displacements=zeros(ndof,1);
        displacements(activeDof)=U;
% stresses at elements
for i=1:nel
indice=ielem(i,:);
elementDof=[indice(1)*2-1 indice(1)*2 indice(2)*2-1 indice(2)*2] ;
xa=xx(indice(2))-xx(indice(1));
ya=yy(indice(2))-yy(indice(1));
length_element=sqrt(xa*xa+ya*ya);
C=xa/length_element;
S=ya/length_element;
sigma(i)=E/length_element*[-C -S C S]*displacements(elementDof);
end
fprintf('The Displacement is')
U
fprintf('The force is')
reactionforce =stiffness*displacements
fprintf('The stress is')
sigma'
```

The Displacement is
U =
0.0320
0.1260
-0.0320
0.1260

The force is
reactionforce =

1.0e+03 *
-2.6667
-1.0000
0
1.0000
0
1.0000
2.6667
-1.0000
The stress is
ans =
1.0e+03 *

4.0000
5.0000
-5.0000
0
-4.0000
0

7.2.4. Strain and Stress of 1D bar Using FEM

Example (60): Find the displacement, the force at the left and the right reactions, and the stress using FEM
When the axial load is subjected P=1000N and E=207GPa.

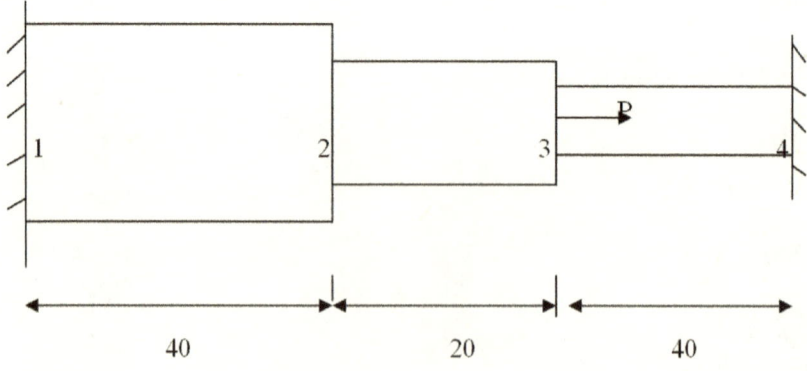

```
clear all
clc
global K u X
format long
n=4; % Number of nodes
for i=1:n
E(i)=207e9;
end
A(1)=5e-4; A(2)=3e-4;A(3)=1e-4;
L(1)=0.4;L(2)=0.3;L(3)=0.4;
L_t=L(1)+L(2)+L(3);
H=L_t/(n+1);
x(1)=0;
for i=2:n
x(i)=x(i-1)+H;
end
K=zeros(n,n);
K(1,1)=E(1)*A(1)/L(1);
K(1,2)=-E(1)*A(1)/L(1);
u=zeros(n,1); % Initialization of the displacement
% Displacement of the Boundary conditions
u(1)=0; % Fixed Geometry at LHS
u(n)=0; % Fixed Geometry at RHS
%---- Build up the Global Stiffness Matrix -------
for i=2:n-1
K(i,i-1)=-(A(i-1)*E(i-1))/L(i-1);
K(i,i)=(A(i-1)*E(i-1))/L(i-1)+(A(i)*E(i))/L(i);
K(i,i+1)=-(A(i)*E(i))/L(i); % Internal Forces
end
K(n,n)=-A(n-1)*E(n-1)/L(n-1);
K(n,n-1)=A(n-1)*E(n-1)/L(n-1);
K1=K(2:n-1,2:n-1);
F=[0 2000]';
Z= K1\F;
% THE REACTION FORCE AT WALL A AND WALL B
FA=A(1)*E(1)/L(1)*Z(1); % in Newton
FB=A(n-1)*E(n-1)/L(n-1)*Z(2); % in Newton
% FOR CHEACKING
F_load=FA+FB;
```

fprintf('The Displacement is')
fprintf('\n \n Z, ')
Z;
The reaction forces are
F_1= 1379.31N (the left reaction force)
F_4 = 620.6 N (the right reaction force)
The displacements are

u_2=5.33066799933367×10^{-6}m
u_3=1.19940029985008×10^{-5} m

APPENDIX

MATLAB Commands and their Meaning

Table: Important MATLAB Commands

Commands Section	MATLAB Commands	Meaning
Matrices Commands	blkdiag ()	Construct a block diagonal matrix.
	diag ()	The diagonal of a matrix command.
	trace ()	To compute the sum of the elements in the main diagonal.
	trill ()	Return to the lower triangle part of a matrix.
	triu ()	Return to the upper triangle part of a matrix.
	det ()	To compute the magnitude of a matrix.
	inv (), rank ()	To compute the inverse of a matrix, and rank of a matrix.
Plotting Commands	plot()	To plot single plotting or data series plotting
	plotyy()	To plot a graph with y-axes on both left and right side.
	plotmatrix()	To plot a matrix.
	fplot ()	To plot mathematical functions.
	plotv(M,T)	To plot vectors as lines from the origin.
	plotsvec (x,c,M)	To plot vectors w/ different colors.
	grid on	To create a graphical sheet.
	hold on	To hold some data or figures.
	set (gca,....,......)	To set color of line, shape, and names.
	bar()	To plot a bar chart.
	bar3()	To plot a 3D bar chart.
	bar3h ()	To plot a 3D bar chart in horizontal.
	barh ()	To plot a single bar chart in horizontal.
	candle ()	To plot a candle chart.
	chartft ()	To plot an interactive display.
	highlow ()	For high-low plotting.

Conditional and for loop commands	**if** logical expression statements **end**	For single statements (true or false condition)
	if expression statements1 **else** statements2 **end**	For double statements.
	if expression1 statements1 **elseif** expression2 statements2 **end**	Double expressions with two conditions.
	for variable = expression statements **end**	Do loop statement.
Digital and Signal Analysis	svd()	To show a singular value decomposition.
	eigshow()	To show the value of a vector from the original.
	ftt()	To compute discrete Fourier transform of a signal.
	ifft()	To compute the inverse Fourier transform of a signal.
	fft2 ()	2D discrete Fourier transform of a signal.
	fftn ()	nD discrete Fourier transform of a signal.
	ifft2()	To compute 2D the inverse Fourier transform of a signal.
	ifftn ()	To compute nD the inverse Fourier transform of a signal.
	abs ()	Magnitude.
	angle ()	To compute the phase angle.
	unwrap()	To put a phase angle in radians.

Interpolations, Integrations, and differential Functions commands	interp1 ()	To compute one-dimensional interpolation.
	interp2 ()	To compute two-dimensional interpolation.
	interp3()	To compute three-dimensional interpolation.
	interpft ()	To compute one-dimensional interpolation using FFT method.
	interpn ()	To compute n-dimensional interpolation (table lookup).
	rand ()	To compute a random element.
	EraseMode	To show an animated gragh.
	int()	To compute limited or unlimited integrations.
	dde23 ()	To compute initial value problems for delay differential equations with constant delays.
	deval ()	To evaluate the numerical solution using the output of dde23.
	ddeset ()	To create/alter the DDE options structure.
	ddeget ()	To extract properties from options structure created with ddeset.
	dsolve()	To compute single or several differential functions.

References

[1]. William J. Palm III, Introduction for MATLAB for Engineers, MacGraw Hill 2005.

[2]. Moler,Cleve," Floating points", MATLAB news and notes, Fall,1996.

[3]. Moler et at. Numerical computing with MATLAB, S.I.A.M,1996.

[4]. Karam et al. Complex Chebyshev Approximation for FIR filter design, IEEE trans. On circuits and systems II. March 1995,pages 207-216

[5]. Brain et al. A guide to MATLAB for Beginners and Experienced users, Cambridge, 2nd edition

[7]. Vinay K. et al. Digital signal processing using MATLAB,McGraw Hill 2009.